FOR JOE, A MAN OF QUIET COURAGE.
HE WOULD HAVE CHOPPED DOWN THE HANGING TREE.

TABLE OF CONTENTS

WHO'S WHO

ACCUSERS

CHURCHILL, Sarah: about 20 years old; a refugee; worked as a servant for George Jacobs Sr. Tried to recant but no one believed her.

HOBBS, Abigail: 14 years old; confessed to witchcraft and then accused others, including both her parents.

HUBBARD, Elizabeth: 16 years old; an orphan who lived with her uncle, Dr. William Griggs.

JOHN INDIAN: age unknown; Indigenous man enslaved by Samuel Parris; husband of Tituba.

LEWIS, Mercy: 19 years old; an orphan and a refugee twice; a live-in servant to the Putnams.

PARRIS, Betty: 9 years old; daughter of Reverend Parris; had an older brother and younger sister, but was the only Parris child to be bewitched; never attended a trial.

PUTNAM, Ann: 12 years old; had nine younger siblings; only accuser who lived at home and had both her parents. Daughter of Thomas and Ann Sr.

PUTNAM, Ann Sr.: about 30 years old; Ann's mother and Thomas's wife.

PUTNAM, Thomas: 44 years old; a veteran of fighting against Indigenous people; militia sergeant; supported Reverend Parris; swore out the first charges.

WALCOTT, Mary: 16 years old; lived with the Putnams; made more accusations than anyone else.

WARREN, Mary: 20 years old; servant to John and Elizabeth Proctor; she was an accuser, recanted, and was herself accused, then became an accuser again.

WILLIAMS, Abigail: 11 years old; orphaned niece of Reverend Parris, lived in his household; the first to be bewitched.

ACCUSED

BISHOP, Bridget: early 50s; wife of a sawyer; lived in Salem Town and didn't know her accusers.

BURROUGHS, George: 42 years old; had been Salem Village's minister; father of seven; unusually strong.

CARRIER, Martha: late 30s; sister to Mary Toothaker.

CLOYCE, Sarah: 44 years old; sister of Rebecca Nurse and Mary Esty.

COREY, Giles: about 80 years old; farmer; husband of Martha.

COREY, Martha: 60s; third wife of Giles.

ENGLISH, Philip: 42 years old; wealthy Salem Town merchant; husband to Mary.

ENGLISH, Mary: about 40 years old; wife to Philip.

ESTY, Mary: 58 years old; sister of Rebecca Nurse and Sarah Cloyce; mother of seven.

GOOD, Dorothy: 4 or 5 years old; daughter of Sarah Good, who was one of the first to be accused.

GOOD, Sarah: 38 years old; disagreeable beggar with a tendency to mutter; had first examination; mother of Dorothy Good.

HOAR, Dorcas: 58 years old; widow; history of theft.

HOWE, Elizabeth: early 50s; related to the Nurses; her husband was blind.

JACOBS, George Sr.: 81 years old; farmer; illiterate.

JACOBS, Margaret: 17 years old; granddaughter of George Sr.; confessed and then recanted.

MARTIN, Susannah: 71 years old; widow from Amesbury.

NURSE, Rebecca: 71 years old; nearly deaf; impeccable reputation; had strong support from her family.

OSBORNE, Sarah: about 49 years old; married a younger man and scandalized the neighbors; had a legal dispute with some of the Putnams.

PROCTOR, Elizabeth: 41 years old; pregnant at time of trial; had five children and six stepchildren; wife to John.

PROCTOR, John: 60 years old; tavern keeper and farmer; husband of Elizabeth; first man accused.

TITUBA: age unknown; enslaved by Samuel Parris; Indigenous woman from Barbados; made the first confession; wife of John Indian.

TOOTHAKER, Mary: 44 years old; widow; sister of Martha Carrier.

WILDS, Sarah: mid-60s; from Topsfield; carpenter's wife; mother of town constable.

WILLARD, John: about 30 years old; Salem Village deputy constable; abusive husband disliked by his in-laws.

OTHERS

CORWIN, Jonathan: 52 years old; Salem Town merchant; justice of the peace; friend of John Hathorne.

DANFORTH, Thomas: 69 years old; deputy governor, Charlestown landowner.

GRIGGS, William, Dr.: 71 years old; Salem Village's doctor.

HATHORNE, John: 51 years old; wealthy magistrate; relative of the Putnams.

HERRICK, George: 30s; Salem deputy sheriff; an upholsterer.

INGERSOLL, Nathaniel: 60 years old; owned tavern where some hearings—and lots of gossip—took place.

MATHER, Cotton: 29 years old; Boston minister; son of Increase; wrote *Wonders of the Invisible World*.

MATHER, Increase: 53 years old; Boston minister; father of Cotton; Harvard College president, 1685–1701; procured new charter for Massachusetts Bay Colony.

PARRIS, Samuel: 39 years old; minister of Salem Village church; sometime court clerk; father of Betty; uncle of Abigail Williams.

SEWALL, Samuel: about 40 years old; Bostonian; judge.

SIBLEY, Mary: 32 years old; neighbor of the Parris family; oversaw baking the witch cake.

INTRODUCTION

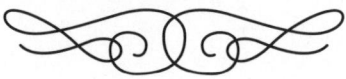

The Salem Witch Trials may be the greatest true crime story in history.

Starting in 1692, neighbors in the Massachusetts Bay Colony pointed accusing fingers at neighbors, and Salem's jail filled. When the witch hunt came to an end, it left behind nineteen nooses swinging in the wind, a pile of rocks used to crush a man to death, two dead dogs, ruined lives, and a legacy of fear.

Was a community that tried to be the best of people attacked by the worst of evil? Or did it commit the vilest crimes? Who were the victims? Who were the criminals?

The word *Salem* still makes the hairs on the back of our necks prickle and causes us to glance over our shoulders. Is anyone there? Waiting in the dark? Watching?

Salem still scares us for a reason: It could happen again.

CHAPTER ONE

THE GIRLS WHO CRIED WITCH

Scoot in closer before I start. It's been more than three centuries, but this story still gives me the creeps.

It started with a prickle. Abigail Williams felt it first. She was a blond eleven-year-old living in Salem, a town in Massachusetts Bay Colony about twenty miles from Boston. Abigail thought someone was pinching her, but no one was there. She felt someone bite her, but she was alone. Her skin burned. Her body shook and shuddered. Her limbs went rigid or slack and uncontrolled. Sometimes she spun around. She said things that made no sense. She shouted and barked or fell silent, unable to talk. Abigail Williams crawled under chairs.

Within a few days her nine-year-old cousin, Betty Parris, had the same symptoms. Abigail lived with Betty and Betty's older brother, Thomas, and younger sister, Susannah. Abigail's own parents had died and her uncle and aunt, Reverend Samuel and Elizabeth Parris, had taken her in. Reverend Parris seems to have been something of a grump, and his wife was chronically ill and unable to keep up with the household.

The Parris family had moved to Salem in 1689. Reverend Parris was born in London, had been wealthy and expected success, yet fell on hard times—and his fall was spectacular. He'd inherited a lot of money and a sugar plantation in Barbados, but Parris turned out to be a lousy plantation manager. He moved to Boston, where he was an even lousier businessman. Taking a job preaching in Salem was a huge letdown for Reverend Parris.

Once the family was settled in Salem Village, Reverend Parris's first problem wasn't witches—that came later. Right away he became embroiled in a dispute with his congregation over his firewood supply. You heard that right. The village was supposed to provide Reverend Parris with a certain number of logs, and he wasn't getting them.

Parris wouldn't let the issue go. He took it to the pulpit, preaching apocalyptic sermons about a coming war of good versus evil, about people who pretended to be good but were really working with the Devil. He planted in the minds of his Puritan congregation the fearsome idea that people in their midst were not what they seemed and couldn't be trusted. Maybe he was just mad about not getting his firewood, but Reverend Parris prepared people to suspect that witches were in their midst. And his congregation believed him.

Reverend Parris could have gotten his firewood by cutting down the Hanging Tree. But he didn't. And it stood waiting.

THE CASE OF GOODY GLOVER

Who were these firewood hoarders in Massachusetts Bay Colony? They were Puritans, a Protestant group that sailed from England in 1630 during a period of religious wars. They believed in a stern God, opposed playing music or games, and took their religion very seriously. And they believed in witches.

You don't. Right?

In 1648 Boston hanged Margaret Jones, who'd been charged with several offenses, including causing deafness and giving people medicines that had terrible effects. The same hour Jones was hanged, a big storm hit Connecticut. Puritans believed God used disasters and illnesses to punish people, so they thought the storm was proof Jones had been guilty. They could have concluded that Jones was innocent and God was angry at them for hanging her, but they didn't.

But there was a weirder case only four years before Abigail Williams began to thrash.

In the summer of 1688, four children of John Goodwin, a Boston mason, began having fits that included barking at each other. Martha, thirteen, had her first fit after an argument with Goody Ann Glover, an Irish Catholic widow who worked for the family. (*Goody* as a title for a married woman was short for *Goodwife*.) Three younger siblings started having fits, too, and accused Goody Glover of tormenting them with witchcraft. Goody Glover was arrested—and hanged as a witch!

The Goodwin children accused more people of being witches, but there were no more arrests. Perhaps no one else was as easy a victim as Ann Glover?

An influential young minister in Boston, Reverend Cotton Mather, who at one point took Martha Goodwin into his home to try to cure her, wrote about the Goodwins in *Memorable Providences, Relating to Witchcraft and Possessions*, which sold very well. So the Goodwins' story became quite well-known throughout New England. Abigail Williams and Betty Parris probably heard all about it. Could they—for fun? for attention?—have imitated the Goodwins' symptoms?

The fact that Reverend Mather had taken Martha in to live with him was significant. His father, Increase Mather, was also a famous minister. The Mathers were celebrities! Abigail and Betty lived in a cramped house and were expected to do endless chores. Maybe they thought they'd be taken to the big city if they had fits. Would a famous family take *them* in? Every kid in Salem would die of envy! Could Abigail and Betty have faked being bewitched, knowing that witchcraft was a capital crime? Anyone convicted of witchcraft would be *hanged*. Could the girls have taken that chance . . . because they wanted a vacation?

THE EGG WHITE SAYS YOU'RE GOING TO DIE

Two other adults lived in the Parris household: an Indigenous woman, Tituba, and her husband, John Indian. We don't know much about Tituba or John Indian, except that they were enslaved people and Reverend Parris had brought Tituba from Barbados to Massachusetts with him.

Because Tituba was from the Caribbean, some people think she must've taught Betty and Abigail about voodoo and Caribbean magic beliefs. There's no proof of this, though. People speculate Tituba knew about the occult because Betty and Abigail may have dabbled with a form of divination—foretelling the future—which went against everything the Puritans believed and which they would've thought was dangerously close to witchcraft.

Today we call the method of divination they used *oomancy*, but they would have called it a Venus glass, Venus being the planet associated

with love. The Venus glass worked by filling a glass with water, then dribbling an egg white into it. Whatever shape the egg white took indicated a girl's future husband's profession and could give a clue to his identity. For example, if the egg white took the shape of a hammer, he'd be a carpenter; if it took the shape of a ship, he'd be a sailor.

When Abigail and Betty dropped their egg white into the water, it took on the shape of a coffin. One of them wouldn't live long enough to marry! Surely this would have upset the girls, but it would be tough to talk to your dad about it when he was Reverend Parris, thundering about the Devil for five hours every Sunday.

What if you felt guilty and believed you were now a bad kid? And if you thought you were going to die young, but couldn't tell anyone, because you couldn't explain how you knew, that might just be reason enough to act like you were being tortured by dark forces—just like the Goodwin kids in Boston. If that's what happened, and Betty and Abigail were hoping that someone would comfort them and say everything would be okay, they really miscalculated.

Could that be how it started? Could the pricks and pinches the girls felt have come from their own guilty consciences? Absolutely. But *did* they? That's one of Salem's many dark mysteries that went to the grave with the girls.

Reverend John Hale from the nearby town of Beverly was an eyewitness to some of the events at Salem and wrote an account published later that recorded Reverend Parris's reaction to the attack on his family. He wrote that Parris consulted local physicians, but the girls' symptoms grew worse. Dr. William Griggs was unable to diagnose them and decided their symptoms had a supernatural cause: "At length one Physician gave his opinion, that they were under an

Evil Hand. This the Neighbours quickly took up, and concluded they were bewitched."

Witchcraft!

If the fits were an indication of God's displeasure, it would have been especially embarrassing to Reverend Parris that divine wrath was aimed at his own family. And if the girls were faking the symptoms to upset him, it worked. Without any medical diagnosis or treatment options, Reverend Parris relied on fasting and prayer to try to heal the girls.

But someone else had another solution: urine.

CHAPTER TWO

LET THEM EAT WITCH CAKE

If you remember one thing from this chapter, let it be this: Devil's food cake and witch cake are not the same thing.

A neighbor, Mary Sibley, wanted to help the girls, so on February 25 she directed John Indian and Tituba to bake a "witch cake," a traditional witch-reveal method from England. The cake was made by mixing the urine of someone presumed to be under a witch's spell with rye flour, then baking the resulting batter in ashes. Then the witch cake was fed to a dog, which was supposed to, somehow, indicate who was bewitching the urinators—or possibly even say the witch's name.

Tituba and John Indian baked a witch cake with Abigail and Betty's urine. But there's no record the dog who ate the cake talked. The result isn't recorded at all. The only thing the test seems to have shown is that a dog will eat absolutely anything!

Reverend Parris was furious when he learned about the witch cake. He called out Mary Sibley in front of the whole congregation in the middle of a church service. He said she had gone "to the Devil for help against the Devil." (He meant the Devil might have caused the girls' fits, but getting answers from a witch cake also relied on paranormal powers.) "Diabolical means was used by the making of a cake by my Indian man, who had his direction from this our sister Mary Sibley: Since which apparitions have been plenty, and exceeding much mischief hath followed. But by this means [it seems] the Devil hath been raised amongst us, and his Rage is vehement and terrible, & when he shall be silenced the Lord only knows." Goody Sibley apologized for her error in judgment.

By the time Reverend Parris announced the Devil had been raised among them, the girls' fits had been going on for several weeks. Reverend Parris's nerves were on edge. He had two contorting, barking children in a small house and he needed quiet to write his sermons. His firewood delivery was spotty. His fence was in bad shape, his pasture weedy. His congregation looked around the meetinghouse during his sermons instead of paying attention and they threw walnuts from the galleries. The doctor was no help and *the Devil walked amongst them.*

Reverend Parris needed answers. Fast. He gathered influential men from Salem and some area ministers at his house. They questioned Abigail and Betty. That must have been intimidating for the girls—but also exciting. They certainly weren't used to adults taking such an interest in them. Now the most important men in the area were asking them questions and listening carefully to their answers. Who wouldn't enjoy that? Who wouldn't want to keep it going?

Reverend Hale attended the gathering and wrote, "[Abigail and

Betty] were bitten and pinched by invisible agents; their arms, necks, and backs turned this way and that way, and returned back again, so as it was impossible for them to do [by] themselves, and beyond the power of any epileptic fits, or natural disease to effect." The girls put on quite the show for the assembled guests that day.

The men ultimately agreed with Dr. Griggs that the "hand of Satan" was behind the fits. This was a critical turning point in the Salem case, although people may not have realized it at the time. It had started with the girls suspecting that they were bad—having guilty consciences because of the Venus glass, or just rebelling against the restrictions of Puritan life. But now the focus was on the girls as victims of attacks by *witches*. They were victims of a *crime*. And once there's a crime, there must be a criminal—and there must be punishment. The search for someone to blame had begun.

WE REPLACED YOUR FACE WITH A TREE

Finding a culprit didn't take any time at all—*the girls named names.*

The witch pinching them, pricking them with needles, and causing their screaming fits? Plot twist! The witch was in their own house!

Tituba!

We don't know why Abigail and Betty named Tituba. Maybe the men had pressured them for a name and they needed to provide one or be accused of faking. Could Tituba's name have come to mind because she was standing right there? Maybe naming her seemed safe—Tituba was enough of an outsider that they could accuse her, but enough of a family member they couldn't imagine anything really bad happening to her. The girls weren't yet fourteen and were therefore too young to testify in court, so maybe naming Tituba seemed free of consequences. As an enslaved woman, Tituba couldn't do anything about the allegations against her, and the assembled men couldn't act on the allegation because the girls weren't of legal age. Witchcraft cases required a trial, like any other crime.

Abigail and Betty may also have named Tituba because she was an "Indian." Puritans believed Indigenous people worshipped the Devil, and they were afraid of both. Massachusetts (which at the time included the district of Maine) had faced bloody conflicts with a number of Indigenous nations and no town was unaffected by the losses. It's likely Abigail's parents were killed in a raid before the Parrises took her in, and now there were rumors of renewed fighting on the horizon. Fear hung like fog over Salem Village.

Massachusetts Bay Colony also faced political uncertainty. The colony had gotten its start in 1629 when King Charles I gave a charter to a group of English Puritan merchants who founded Massachusetts Bay Colony. (There were already Indigenous nations living there, but they weren't consulted, and their presence didn't stop the king from giving away their land.)

The charter outlined laws by which the colonists had to abide, but as time went on, the colonists began to ignore some of the laws that cost them money or didn't match their strict religious beliefs. For example, the Puritans weren't supposed to fine people who celebrated Christmas, but they did—the celebrants had to pay five shillings (about $76.00 today) per person if they took the day off work or had a feast! In addition, after Charles I's son took the throne as Charles II, he learned that instead of using English coins that had his picture on them, the colonists were making coins themselves—and putting a picture of a pine tree where his face should have gone. Plenty irritated, Charles II revoked the whole charter in 1684.

This gave Massachusetts Bay Colony problems, not the least of which was that without a charter, the Colony's legal system couldn't operate, because it didn't have England's royal approval anymore. Which meant no court trials could be held. Which meant anyone in jail awaiting trial had to just keep waiting.

On top of all that, King Charles II died in early 1685. The new king, James II, was Catholic. In 1688 Protestant King William and Queen Mary seized the English throne and James II fled the country. This was the "Glorious Revolution." The Puritans were glad William and Mary won the power struggle, because they didn't like Catholics. They took the opportunity to get rid of a hated governor, then sent Reverend Increase Mather to London to try to get the charter reinstated. No one knew if he could do it, and at best it would take months. The government had broken down. Did anyone in England have their backs? It must have been nerve-racking—even before reports of witchcraft.

Still, Abigail and Betty naming Tituba as the witch torturing them seems like a shocking betrayal. She ate with the Parrises, probably slept in the same space as the children, attended Reverend Parris's twice-a-day prayers along with the rest of the family, and joined them at the hearth to sing psalms. How could the girls be so cruel to someone they presumably knew well? Witchcraft was punishable by death. If you accused someone of witchcraft and they *hadn't* bewitched you, you weren't a victim. If things got out of hand and the adults believed you, you could be a *murderer*.

As soon as the girls named Tituba, the men at Parris's home questioned her. She admitted to baking the witch cake under the direction of Goody Sibley. She denied being a witch, but then said that in Barbados she'd known a witch who'd taught her a little protective magic. Aha! But did the men ask Tituba why she would have baked a witch cake—which was designed to expose a witch—if she actually *was* one? Nope.

As they left the gathering, under a moon that hung larger and lower in the sky than usual, Reverend Parris's visitors cautioned him against rash action and advised him not to do anything yet, but to wait and pray.

The Putnams were going to make that impossible.

THREE FAMILIES, TWO TOWNS

The same day Abigail and Betty said Tituba was the witch causing their fits, their twelve-year-old neighbor, Ann Putnam, began to shake and convulse. She went rigid and limp, shouted wild things, or lost the ability to speak at all. She had the same symptoms as Abigail and Betty—Ann Putnam was also "under an evil hand." Deep in the New England winter, witchcraft symptoms were spreading.

In many ways, the macabre events in Salem are the story of three families: the Parrises, the Putnams, and the Porters. Just as Reverend Parris had fallen on hard times, the Putnams had also crashed. Ann's great-grandfather, John, left England and by 1640 had settled in Salem, where he amassed almost eight hundred acres of land. He left it to his sons, and they prospered. But when they built an ironworks, an angry employee burned the place down, and the land was subdivided again among John's grandsons' generation, making the holdings much smaller.

As the Putnam family was hitting hard times, the Porters' fortunes were rising. John Porter immigrated from England about the same time as John Putnam, and he amassed the most land of anyone in Salem. Instead of just farmland, however, Porter had waterfront property, which allowed him to build docks and get into the shipping industry. Shipping was the economic future of New England, so Porter's descendants would be set up better than Putnam's.

Envy creates hard feelings. Resentments fester. That's motive.

Like the Parrises, the Putnam family lived in Salem Village; the Porters, however, lived in Salem Town. The two Salems had developed a couple of decades before Abigail, Betty, and Ann claimed to be bewitched. Salem Town was founded first and became a center for commerce and trade. Its residents, like the Porters, embraced economic and cultural change. More vexing, they were getting rich doing it.

Money? That's motive, too.

The Putnams represented the old values of a tight-knit farming community. When they grew unhappy with the bustling commercial hub that Salem Town had become, they split off, along with families that felt the same way, to form Salem Village a few miles away. Salem Village struggled financially and was overshadowed by Salem Town. I saw the community fracture, but I didn't understand what was to come.

Maybe I should have anticipated trouble, because Salem Villagers were a difficult bunch. They had frequent conflicts with their neighbors and with the men they hired to preach in their meetinghouse. A few years before Reverend Parris was hired, Salem Village stopped paying their minister, Reverend George Burroughs, and he left. Because the church hadn't paid him, Burroughs borrowed money from John Putnam to bury his wife, who had just passed away. He returned a few weeks later to meet with village officials, apparently hoping they'd fork over his back pay. Instead of apologizing and giving him the back pay, though, John Putnam had him arrested for debt!

The Putnams weren't easy people to deal with, then, and it got worse when the Porter faction in Salem Town blocked the Putnams from having their Salem Village church become fully credentialed (and not just a branch of Salem Town's church). Salem Town arbitrators told Putnam and his cronies to "desist at present . . . till your spirits are better quieted and composed." That's seventeenth-century talk for "Settle down"—accompanied by an eye roll.

Soon after Salem Village lost its bid to become a full church, the minister left and Salem Village offered the job to Samuel Parris. Thomas Putnam and Samuel Parris were both bitter men who expected more from life than they got. Then their children began to twitch. Reverend Parris could consult local dignitaries all he liked, but Thomas Putnam wasn't going to ask for anyone else's opinions. And he sure wasn't going to just wait and pray about it.

CHAPTER THREE

A WEB OF RELATIONSHIPS

The day Abigail and Betty accused Tituba and Ann Putnam began to convulse, Dr. Griggs's sixteen-year-old niece Elizabeth Hubbard also started to have fits. Ann and Elizabeth didn't wait weeks to name their tormentor, as Abigail and Betty had. They accused not only Tituba but also two more local women of witchcraft: Sarah Good and Sarah Osborne. There were now more accusers—and more accused. The Devil was walking through the streets of Salem!

Thomas Putnam took immediate action. On February 29— a day that doesn't even exist most years—he and his brother, Edward, rode with two friends to Salem Town, where legal charges could be filed. They made two formal complaints of witchcraft—one against Tituba and Sarah Osborne together, and one against Sarah Good—claiming the injured parties to be Betty Parris, Abigail Williams, Ann Putnam, and Elizabeth Hubbard.

That day in 1692, the dark forces in Salem shifted. Salem finally had a victim who was old enough to testify—Elizabeth Hubbard. She'd have heard all about the symptoms of the girls in the Parris household and may well have seen their fits firsthand.

Goody Sarah Good was thirty-eight and had two daughters, an infant and a four-year-old. She'd become poor after two bad marriages, a situation made worse when she didn't receive an inheritance that was rightfully hers. Good was generally angry at the world—and let people know it. She also tended to mutter. People suspected she was mumbling rude things and, because she was odd, assumed she must be dabbling in witchcraft. She had little power in the community, people were already suspicious of her, and nobody much liked her. After Tituba, Goody Good was probably the easiest target in town.

The other accused woman, Sarah Osborne, was forty-nine. After her husband died, she married a young servant, scandalizing Salem Village. She had an ongoing dispute over her first husband's will with its executor—who was Ann Putnam's grandfather! Did a financial dispute with the Putnams make Osborne another easy target? Or a lucrative one?

When Ann's father and uncle rode into Salem Town to file those charges, they found quick allies in two magistrates, John Hathorne and Jonathan Corwin, both in their early fifties. Hathorne was experienced in hearing judicial cases, had an impressive house and six children, and was a prominent person in Salem. Oh, and one more thing—he was related to the Putnams!

Corwin, a longtime ally of Hathorne's, was wealthy and owned several sawmills, some co-owned by Hathorne. They lived a block apart and Hathorne's late brother had been married to Corwin's sister. Corwin was also an ally of Reverend Parris. Once when Parris complained about the congregation not delivering his firewood, Corwin had shown up with a load. So there was a web of relationships among the Parrises, the Putnams, and the legal authorities.

Once formal charges were filed, legal proceedings against the accused witches could begin. Before Massachusetts Bay Colony held a trial for someone charged with a crime, a law enforcement official questioned the suspect in what was called the "examination." Normally, an examination would have been held privately—after all, it was just a fact-finding exercise. If things went badly for the defendant during their examination, they *could* be jailed, but they wouldn't be sentenced until after they were tried and found guilty.

Well, that was the way it was *supposed* to work, the way I'd seen it work before.

For reasons we can only guess, Hathorne and Corwin decided to question the suspects in public. They also decided to keep a record of the proceedings. These were the first indications that the judicial process in Salem was veering off course. Certainly, the magistrates knew everybody in Salem was fascinated by what was going on and that public examinations of witches would be the biggest show in town.

There was another possibility. Because Massachusetts Bay Colony had lost its charter, they couldn't hold trials, and they didn't know how long after the examinations they'd have to wait until a trial could be held. Maybe they wanted to document everything—in front of the community—in case witnesses forgot details or died before a trial started. Whatever their rationale, without the promise of a quick trial, the examinations would become the main event, at least for the foreseeable future. And that turned them into a circus.

CHAPTER FOUR

GOOD AND "EVIL" (AND OSBORNE)

One day later, on Tuesday, March 1, Hathorne and Corwin issued arrest warrants for Tituba, Sarah Good, and Sarah Osborne, and interrogated all three in Salem Village that same day, starting with Goody Good. She arrived at Nathaniel Ingersoll's Tavern at ten o'clock for the examination. A tavern, you ask? Back then taverns didn't have a bad reputation; kids could go in, and on Sundays people stopped for cider and a hot meal before going back to the meetinghouse for the afternoon sermon. Ingersoll's was located conveniently close to the Salem Village meetinghouse and was large enough to accommodate a crowd. But it turns out, not *this* crowd—it grew so much that the proceedings had to be moved into the meetinghouse itself.

The table that usually held bread and wine for communion was dragged in front of the pulpit. The crowd rushed in and grabbed the best seats they could get, instead of sitting in their assigned pews, as they had to do on Sundays. (Rules? What rules?) Ezekiel Cheever, a tailor, was assigned to keep the written record of the examinations. They said a prayer, and Hathorne asked the first question of the first examination: "Sarah Good, what evil spirit have you familiarity with?"

Good replied, "None," but the question must have been chilling for her. She was in a dark meetinghouse (broken windows had been boarded up instead of being repaired), she was standing several feet from her inquisitors with a railing between them, she'd never testified before, and the question itself made it clear Hathorne assumed she was guilty. No surprise there! In seventeenth-century Massachusetts Bay Colony, defendants were presumed guilty and had to prove their innocence.

Hathorne asked his next question: "Have you made no contract with the Devil?"

"No," Good answered.

"Why do you hurt these children?"

When Good replied she didn't hurt the girls, Hathorne asked her what creature she got to do it for her, then. He was expressing the common belief that witches had a *familiar*, often in animal form, that worked with them and did some of their evil work. A demonic sidekick! People believed witches fed their familiars from an extra nipple somewhere on their bodies—and if you examined a witch, you could often find the "witch's mark" where the familiar fed. But it didn't necessarily look like a regular nipple; it could just be a small discoloration or spot. That, of course, was a problem for anybody with a mole or birthmark or rash or pimple anywhere on their body.

Good, who surely felt badgered by that point, replied, "No creature but I am falsely accused."

Hathorne completely ignored her denial, following up with a factual question for the first time. Cheever was scribbling as fast as he could, but he didn't get Hathorne's exact words recorded here. Cheever wrote down his question as, "Why did you go away muttering from mr Paris his house?" This gave Good a problem because she had, in fact, muttered after leaving the Parris home a few weeks earlier. She'd gone there begging with her little girl, Dorothy. After Reverend Parris had given her some food, she turned to go and mumbled something that Parris hadn't heard clearly.

"I did not mutter but I thanked him for what he gave my child." It was a logical explanation—and might have been true—but it didn't help Good.

Hathorne had one more go: "Have you made no contract with the Devil?"

"No."

At that point Hathorne asked the four accusers, who were seated together, to stand up and tell the assembly if Goody Good was the woman who'd hurt them. All four—Abigail, Betty, Ann, and Elizabeth—said yes, Sarah Good had tormented them. Three of the girls said she'd even attacked them just that morning! Then the four of them fell into convulsive fits. The dimly lit meetinghouse must have been in an uproar. Now the whole town could witness their fits—the supposed work of witches—firsthand. Do you suppose people jumped onto the pews to get a better look?

"Sarah Good, do you not see now what you have done?" Hathorne asked over the din. "Why do you not tell us the truth? Why do you thus torment these poor children?"

Good kept her composure. "I do not torment them."

After being harassed a bit longer, Sarah Good reminded the magistrates they'd arrested *three* people. It was a clear attempt to shift blame, and Hathorne took the bait. He demanded to know who, then, caused the convulsions. Good tried to deflect: "I do not know but it was some you brought into the meeting house with you." Finally, when Hathorne asked, "Who is it then that tormented the children?" Good said, "It was Osborne."

Unexpectedly, though, this didn't satisfy Hathorne, who continued to go after Good. If she thought accusing Osborne would save her, she was wrong. Dead wrong.

Hathorne demanded again to know what Good was muttering as she left Reverend Parris's house after begging there. This time, Good said she was reciting a psalm. In extremely religious Massachusetts Bay Colony, that was a good answer—but then Hathorne demanded to know which one. Good paused, then "muttered over some part of a psalm," as Cheever recorded it, without noting which psalm it was. Cheever didn't seem to believe her. Do you? Probably instead of reciting psalms as she left after begging, she was commenting on the lack of generosity of her neighbors, right? But that wouldn't have played well in the packed meetinghouse.

Clearly Sarah Good wasn't getting a fair hearing by any modern standard of justice. In addition to the magistrates presuming she was guilty, even Ezekiel Cheever was deeply biased against her. At the end of his record of Good's interrogation, he wrote, "her answers were in [a] very wicked, spiteful manner . . . with base and abusive words and many lies."

A particularly appalling aspect of the Salem events became apparent in this first examination. When Good's own husband, William, was

called to testify, he turned on his wife! The marriage wasn't great—
perhaps their money problems had taken their toll—but William told the
magistrates he thought his wife probably *was* a witch, or on her way to
becoming one. When Hathorne asked if he'd ever seen his wife perform
witchcraft, he admitted he hadn't, but said, "it was her bad carriage
[behavior] to him" that caused him to accuse her. William was saying
his wife was a witch because he found her hard to get along with! That's
about as clear a case of payback as you can imagine, but the constables
accepted it without question. William Good would not be the last
relative to turn on a family member in that meetinghouse.

THIS ISN'T GOOD.
IT'S OSBORNE.

Goody Sarah Osborne was brought in front of the magistrates. Hathorne
grilled her in the same manner he had Goody Good. Goody Osborne
refused to acknowledge she was a witch. Hathorne asked if she had a
familiar. Osborne said she did not.

"Sarah Good saith that it was you that hurt the children," Hathorne
said.

"I do not know that the Devil goes about in my likeness to do any
hurt."

And with that, Goody Osborne criticized the magistrate's
acceptance of *spectral evidence*. A specter is a ghost or spirit.
Remember at Goody Good's examination when three of the girls
said she'd attacked them that very morning? They didn't mean she'd
physically shown up in their bedrooms and tortured them. They meant
it was her *specter* that had attacked them—invisible to everyone but
the victims. How do you defend yourself against *that*? It beats even an

ironclad alibi, because if two hundred people saw you at the time of an attack across town from where it occurred, that doesn't mean they can account for what your *specter* was up to at the same time. And a specter was invisible to anyone except the person being attacked. Convenient, right?

Once you decided to accept spectral evidence, you had to just believe anything an accuser said. Because how could anybody prove they'd kept body and specter together? Could *you*? Hathorne and Corwin don't seem to have ever made a formal decision to accept spectral evidence. They just did it.

Goody Osborne challenged that—how did they know the Devil hadn't taken her shape? Couldn't he do that? Were they *sure* it was her? Hathorne didn't acknowledge Osborne's statement. He had the four accusers stand up, look her over, and confirm she was one of the women afflicting them. Then an interesting issue came up—that of Goody Osborne's clothes. The girls said they'd "seen her in [the] very habit that she was now in"—in other words, wearing the same clothes—when she had pinched and tormented them. That, too, was taken as proof her specter had appeared to them. Astonishingly, it never occurred to the magistrates the girls could simply be lying.

It occurred to me.

Asked whether she ever heard voices, Osborne admitted she thought she'd once heard a voice suggest she skip church that Sunday, but she went anyway.

"Why did you yield thus far to the Devil as never to go to meeting since?" Hathorne asked, meaning why hadn't she been in church since that time, and was it the Devil keeping her away?

"Alas I have been sick and not able to go."

Well, with that, people in the audience shouted it had been fourteen months since Osborne attended church services. Between her dispute with Putnam over her first husband's will and her judgy neighbors whispering about her second marriage, no wonder she didn't attend church. Who would want to? But she couldn't say that.

The questions about Goody Osborne's church attendance started with a question shouted from the crowd, which Hathorne repeated. A crowd should never have been present in the first place—and shouldn't have been feeding the magistrates questions.

Sarah Good and Sarah Osborne had denied being witches—that was no surprise. But a surprise was coming. Salem's strange tale was about to get a whole lot stranger.

CHAPTER FIVE

TITUBA'S TALES OF TAILS

It was finally time to question Tituba.

Hathorne said, "Tituba, what evil spirit have you familiarity with?"

"None."

"Why do you hurt these children?" (Ah, there's that "guilty until proven innocent" thinking again!)

"I do not hurt them."

"Who is it, then?"

"The Devil for ought I know."

So far, no different from the previous examinations. Then Hathorne asked, "Did you never see the Devil?"

"The Devil came to me and bid me serve him."

Wait! Was Tituba saying she *had* seen the Devil? Even *talked* with him?

"Who have you seen?" Hathorne was asking Tituba to name names.

"Four women sometimes hurt the children."

"Who were they?"

The entire crowd packed into the dark meetinghouse must have leaned forward and held its breath.

Tituba said the four women hurting the children were Sarah Osborne and Sarah Good, plus two women she didn't know.

Hathorne probably had to wait for the din to die down before he could ask if the Devil had asked Tituba to sign his book. "Signing his book" meant you were making a pact with the Devil, which of course was a clear violation of the law against witchcraft.

At first Tituba said no, but then, apparently catching on to what Hathorne wanted from her, she agreed she *had* signed the Devil's book. If she'd signed the book, she might've seen who else had signed the book, and those were names Hathorne would want. Perhaps Tituba felt she had an opportunity here. As an enslaved person, figuring out what someone wanted and agreeing with it may have been a skill she'd learned a long time ago to try to protect herself.

Tituba couldn't read, but Hathorne asked if she'd seen any marks—which functioned as the signature of an illiterate person—in the book in addition to hers, even if she hadn't been able to read them. That would mean more people had made a pact with the Devil. This was potentially really big . . . and Tituba said . . .

Yes! She'd seen eight or nine marks in the Devil's book besides her own.

This was stunning! More witches hiding in their midst! Hathorne suggested that perhaps the Devil had mentioned the names to Tituba. Could she say who they were? Tituba said no, the Devil had just said the names of Sarah Good and Sarah Osborne—oh, and that some of the people lived in Boston. Tituba was giving Hathorne what he wanted to hear, but she avoided accusing anyone who wasn't already in trouble.

Asked once more if she hurt the children, Tituba this time replied, "Yes, but I will hurt them no more."

Asked if she was sorry she'd hurt them, Tituba said simply, "Yes."

Hathorne pressed her to explain why she harmed them. "They say hurt children or we will do worse to you," Tituba replied. This was a phrase she repeated a number of times.

Tituba confessed! To being a witch! But *why*?

WE RIDE UPON STICKS

She said later that Reverend Parris had beaten her until she agreed to confess to witchcraft. That would certainly explain why she'd say she bewitched the girls—but not why she denied being a witch at the beginning of her examination. Her affection for Betty Parris comes through in her testimony, though, and Tituba had joined the family before Betty had been born. Maybe she just didn't want to say she'd hurt Betty.

And don't forget—Tituba had the advantage of seeing how things had gone for Sarah Good and Sarah Osborne in their examinations. Tituba had never been in trouble before; she appears in no court records prior to the witch hunt. Since asserting innocence didn't seem to work for Goody Good or Goody Osborne, could she have made a bold gamble to try to please Hathorne by giving him what he asked for—a confession, and a corroboration of the town's worst fear—that there were more witches out there? There she was, an enslaved woman surrounded by an overflow crowd shifting with impatience while the afflicted girls contorted for all to see. Maybe it was just easier to confess and get it over with.

There's another possibility, though. What if Tituba thought the allegation against her was *true*? Her neighbor, Goody Sibley, had persuaded Tituba and her husband to bake that witch cake, which was an attempt at paranormal divination. Hathorne didn't ask Tituba about the witch cake, but Reverend Parris had been furious about it. Under the weight of all the questions, and with the guilt of the witch cake on her conscience, maybe Tituba thought she *had* performed witchcraft. If everybody else was convinced she was a witch—maybe they were right.

If Reverend Parris *did* beat Tituba to make her confess, what was his motive? We'll never know, but the fact the afflictions started in his own home must have been a factor. Shifting the question from *What is wrong with the girls?* to *What has been done to the girls?* was an important distinction, and it may have helped Reverend Parris preserve his standing in the village.

Pummeled by questions from the magistrates, Tituba even confessed to seeing all sorts of paranormal creatures. Goody Good, she said, had a yellow bird that suckled between her fingers as her familiar! And Goody Osborne had two familiars, one that was two or three feet tall, covered in hair, and walked upright, and one with a woman's head, two legs, and wings. Tituba said she'd seen strange beasts, including a black cat, two red cats, a hog, and a "great black dog."

When Hathorne asked Tituba about gatherings of witches, she said witches were able to travel long distances because "We ride upon sticks and are there presently." Tituba had just claimed a frightening new power for witches in New England. They could show up anytime, anyplace, because they could *fly*. Cool superpower—really bad timing for claiming it, though.

Those God-fearing Puritans of Salem must have been beside themselves during Tituba's testimony. The four afflicted girls certainly were affected—they'd been writhing and thrashing, but when Tituba started to confess, they calmed right down, listening with rapt attention along with everybody else.

And what she said was gripping: Goody Good had visited the Parris family during their prayer one evening, a yellow bird and a black cat with her, and she'd covered Tituba's ears to keep her from hearing the scriptures. And a man in a dark coat had once visited her—not someone from Salem, but from the "other world." He'd threatened to cut off Tituba's head if she told anyone about him.

Now, let's think about this a moment: As a minister, Reverend Parris would have worn a dark coat. And Tituba said he'd beaten her to get her to agree to confess. Could Tituba have been spinning fanciful stories from things that had really happened to her?

On and on Tituba went, providing more and more details as she spun her tale—the man in black clothes was tall, a female witch wore a white hood and a black hood. If nothing else, Tituba had a great imagination. As her examination came to an end, the four girls began to convulse again. Fascinatingly, Tituba also began to have a fit, and Hathorne asked if she could see who was attacking her.

"Yes it is Goody Good."

Immediately the girls agreed it was Goody Good causing their convulsions. How angry must Sarah Good have been? She was always irritated about something—but this accusation, when she was sitting right there in the meetinghouse? What could she possibly say to defend herself?

Then Tituba said Good's attack had temporarily blinded her and that she was unable to speak. Tituba had grabbed her opportunity to move from being a defendant to a victim, decided her examination was over, and managed to stop it.

Hathorne and Corwin (who'd been a silent presence the whole time) had heard enough. They sent Goody Osborne and Tituba to the big stone prison in Boston, where'd they stay for an indefinite amount of time since no trials were being held. With her infant daughter, Goody Good was sent to the nearby Ipswich jail, riding behind Constable Joseph Herrick on his horse. Three times she jumped off the horse and made a run for it. Each time Herrick caught her. She would later be transferred to the Boston prison, too.

Hathorne visited Tituba in jail four times, on March 2, 3, 5, and 7, to ask more questions. Tituba cheerfully spun off further details— vibrantly colored birds, fantastical beasts, and meetings of witches flying on sticks through the night. She created a remarkably vivid world, in contrast with slushy late-winter Salem with its leaden skies and the rough gray bark of the Hanging Tree.

CHAPTER SIX

PUTNAM IN PURSUIT

Three women accused of witchcraft were in jail. Salem held its collective breath. Was this the end of it? Were they now safe from flying witches who pinched their children and poked them with pins?

For a brief, precarious moment, things seemed to calm down. Immediately after the examinations, Salem Village held a town meeting to deal with ordinary town business. It must've been a relief to focus on issues of everyday life, such as Salem Town's offer to let Salem Village avoid its road maintenance responsibilities. In return, Salem Village would provide financial help to the village poor. (Salem Village refused.)

That calm was the eye of the hurricane.

On the night of March 3, the village cooper (barrel maker) and a worker saw a weird-looking animal that they said turned into two or three women who flew away.

They thought Goody Good was involved. Even though she was locked away in jail, her specter could still cause trouble. What the men saw sounds like a dream, or something they "saw" after a night drinking at the tavern. Maybe it was. But whatever it was, it came from a prickle-necked fear of things that go bump in the night—that something is out there, and it might be coming.

As for Abigail Williams, Betty Parris, and Elizabeth Hubbard? Funny enough—or not so funny, really—they stopped having fits as soon as the three women they'd accused were hauled off to jail. For a time, only Ann Putnam continued to be afflicted. And it was because of her that the witch scare didn't end with those examinations on March 1. It spun on because of fear—and because of Ann's father, Thomas Putnam.

I know. I was there.

I DON'T KNOW WHAT YOU'RE WEARING, BUT YOU'RE STILL A WITCH

The records from the Salem witch trials tell us a lot, including when the pace of accusations slowed. The first half of March was quiet. On March 11, Reverend Parris held a prayer meeting at his house and Betty and Abigail had fits but made no accusations. Parris sent Betty—but not Abigail—to Salem Town to stay with the family of his friend Stephen Sewall. Maybe Parris was more worried about his daughter than his niece. Maybe he couldn't find someone to take Abigail. We'll never know. Staying with Sewall separated Betty from the other girls, and her fits gradually stopped. Yet no one thought to separate the other girls?

On Saturday, March 12, Ann Putnam accused Martha Corey of appearing to her as a specter and tormenting her. Goody Corey was an intelligent woman and a member of the church. Not everyone who attended church was a member. Becoming a church member was a bit of an ordeal, but those people who went through it earned a higher status in the community. Goody Corey had that status, which you'd think would have made her less likely to be accused of being a witch. Think again.

Goody Corey may have been a church member, but she was also known to be a skeptic about all the witchcraft allegations in Salem. She'd said publicly she didn't think there were any witches in town, despite the afflicted girls' claims. In fact, when her husband, Giles, saddled his horse to ride to the examinations, Goody Corey yanked the saddle off to prevent him from going! She had an analytical mind, and her doubts made her dangerous to anyone who wanted to keep the witchcraft scare going.

Was anyone trying to keep the scare going? And who might benefit from it? The accusations against Tituba, Sarah Good, and Sarah Osborne could be chalked up to hysteria and the need to find some explanation for the weird things happening in the Parris home. But after that, when the whole scare could've ended, to have a skeptic like Goody Corey accused? Now the door was open to use witchcraft charges to bully other people.

To win property disputes by forcing enemies into line—or silencing them.

To settle old scores.

To make victims dangle from a noose the way a trapped fly dangles from a line of spider silk.

There was a web of connections among the people who would keep the trials going—and Thomas Putnam was the spider sitting in the middle of it.

Still, when Ann made her accusation and before they took action, the adult Putnams made some effort to verify Ann's claims. Ann's uncle Edward and another man asked Ann what dress Goody Corey was wearing when her specter appeared, figuring they could check her story by riding to Corey's house to see if she was wearing the dress Ann described. Ann dodged the question, explaining Goody Corey's specter had temporarily blinded her because she knew the men would check on her clothing. Quick thinking on Ann's part? Did she come up with that excuse herself? Or did her father? We'll never know.

The men headed over to Goody Corey's on March 12, even though they had no proof whatsoever to verify Ann's accusations. She was home alone and received them pleasantly. She said she knew they were there to question her about being a witch, but that she wasn't one. Goody Corey asked if Ann had told them what she was wearing when she allegedly attacked the girl. This wasn't a strange question for her to ask—Tituba had described the clothing worn by the witches she saw, and people probably realized that could help identify them.

When the men explained that the specter had blinded Ann, Goody Corey smiled, probably thinking this was obviously the girl's way to avoid being caught in a lie. But if Martha Corey was relieved, she shouldn't have been. The men thought she smiled because she couldn't be identified by her clothes—and thought she'd tricked them.

On March 14, Goody Corey returned the Putnams' visit, apparently to confront Ann about her accusations. Ann claimed she saw Corey's familiar, a yellow bird sucking between Goody Corey's fingers, and went into a fit.

So did the Putnams' servant, Mercy Lewis! Mercy was nineteen years old, making her the oldest person to be afflicted so far. She had a tragic past. She'd been a refugee twice from the wars with Indigenous people in Maine. Her grandparents, uncles, and cousins had all been killed in an Indigenous attack when she was a toddler, and her parents died in another raid when she was sixteen. Like many of the people who wound up accusing their neighbors of witchcraft, Mercy was deeply traumatized by violence. She may not have had spectral visits from witches, but it's hard to imagine she didn't have nightmares—and a terrible fear of things that go bump in the night.

Four days after that visit, Ann's mother (also named Ann) suddenly had a fit. And just like that, an adult was afflicted. (People in Salem would continue to call the accusers "the afflicted girls" even after the group included adult women and even some men.) Ann Sr. claimed Martha Corey was tormenting her. Goody Corey had clearly become a threat to the Putnams, and unlike her daughter, Ann Sr. was old enough to be a witness once Salem Village could hold trials again. That made her a very dangerous accuser.

On Saturday, March 19, the day after Ann Sr. had her fit, a warrant was issued for Goody Corey's arrest. She was charged with committing acts of "witchcraft and thereby done much hurt and injury unto the bodies of Ann Putnam, the wife of Thomas Putnam . . . Ann Putnam, the daughter of Thomas Putnam, and Mercy Lewis, single woman living in the Putnams' family," along with Abigail Williams and Elizabeth Hubbard.

The warrant couldn't be served on a Sunday—that would violate Puritan religious rules against working on the sabbath. The day after the warrant against her was issued, Goody Corey, showing extraordinary courage, swept into the meetinghouse as church began and settled in her pew for services. The minister at the pulpit that day was not Reverend Parris, but Reverend Deodat Lawson, who'd once served Salem Village and whom Reverend Parris invited to return as a witness to the strange occurrences. Reverend Parris asked him to function as an outside observer, and with his arrival—on the day of Goody Corey's arrest warrant—came the opportunity for Salem Villagers to pause, take a breath, and examine what they were really doing.

But that didn't happen because of Mary Walcott's teeth.

CHAPTER SEVEN

BITING, BEWITCHING, AND BLASPHEMY

As Reverend Lawson was settling into a room at Ingersoll's Tavern on March 19, he was visited by sixteen-year-old Mary Walcott, who'd been one of his young parishioners when he'd been Salem Village's preacher. Why would she be visiting him as soon as he stepped into town? Was there a calculated motive? Oh, you know it.

Mary Walcott and Ann Putnam were close cousins, and Mary spent a lot of time with the Putnams. There's some evidence she may have even lived with them. Mary doesn't seem to have delivered anything to the tavern on March 19, or to have given Reverend Lawson paperwork related to his role as an informal observer. So why *did* she show up? Was Thomas Putnam trying to influence the outside observer? Was the spider spinning its web?

Reverend Lawson and Mary spoke briefly at the door to his room, then suddenly Mary screamed. A specter had bitten her wrist! Lawson got a candle and checked her arm, and sure enough, there were upper and lower teeth marks on her skin. Logic would suggest Mary had bitten herself before knocking on Lawson's door, then screamed to draw his attention to her wrist before the marks faded. If so, Lawson fell for it.

What better way to get Reverend Lawson, the outside observer, on the accusers' side than to have him witness a girl being attacked by a witch right in front of him? The Case of the Bitten Wrist suggests the Putnam faction were scheming schemers indeed.

That "spectral" bite mark would've been fresh on Reverend Lawson's mind when he stood at Salem Village's meetinghouse pulpit the next day. There was Goody Corey in her seat and then Ann Putnam and Abigail Williams started throwing massive fits. They were joined by a thrashing Mary Walcott, Mercy Lewis, and Elizabeth Hubbard, along with two middle-aged women who'd just started having fits, Bathshua Pope and Sarah Bibber. It was a veritable epidemic! I could hear the shrieking across town.

The witchcraft victims began shouting things that sounded less like possession and more like unabashed insolence. Abigail demanded Reverend Lawson say what book of the Bible his text was from before he began a scripture reading. And after he'd read it, she shouted that it had been a long selection. A few minutes into Lawson's sermon, Goody Pope exclaimed, "Now there is enough of that."

They were criticizing the minister, saying he was taking too long and was boring!

That simply wasn't done in a Puritan church, although people may have longed to shout that they were bored as hour after hour of services went by. Now it seemed like the accusers could get away with virtually anything they wanted, even heckling a guest preacher. Normally, the

fine for interrupting a minister was a hefty five pounds (about $1,500 today). But if you declared you didn't want to listen to the next two hours of a sermon and you'd interrupted because you were *bewitched*? Well, that would just make people feel sorry for you. And that's exactly what the accusers achieved. They said the reason for their thrashing, contorting, and shouting at the minister was because Goody Corey was right there bewitching them! It must have been thrilling to get away with that.

A GOSPEL WOMAN

On Monday, March 21, everyone was crammed back in the meetinghouse to see Goody Corey's examination. Hathorne began: "You are now in the hands of Authority. Tell me now why you hurt these persons."

Corey replied, "I do not."

She repeatedly asked to be allowed to pray, but Hathorne refused. "We do not send for you to go to prayer."

Corey could do nothing but protest her innocence. "I am an innocent person: I never had to do with witchcraft since I was born. I am a Gospel Woman."

Hathorne gestured to the afflicted girls. "Do you not see these complain of you?"

Corey courageously replied, "The Lord open the eyes of the magistrates and ministers: The Lord show his power to discover the guilty." Hathorne and Corwin were looking in the wrong direction, she was saying; the guilt wasn't with the accused—but with the accusers!

Ah! Maybe now they were getting somewhere? But not so fast . . .

Hathorne kept on. How had Corey known to ask the men who'd visited her if Ann Putnam had asked what clothes she was wearing when Corey supposedly appeared to the girl as a specter? Before

Corey could even respond, Cheever "interrupted her and bid her not begin with a lie." She hadn't even explained before she was called a liar! Record keepers are meant to be impartial—and silent. Not in Salem, apparently! And then, the record reads, "And so Edward Putnam declared the matter." Corey wasn't allowed to give her testimony—Ann's uncle Edward took over to tell what happened.

Hathorne persisted. Ann hadn't known what Corey was wearing because the specter had blinded her, so how had Corey known to ask about it? She said her husband had told her that in the previous allegations against accused witches, the girls had mentioned their clothes. The magistrate asked Giles Corey if this was true, and *he said that it was not.* Giles also cited several small domestic incidents that made it sound as though he thought his wife could be a witch, like their housecat briefly getting sick. Cheever wrote Martha Corey's name in his record to jot down her response, but it's followed by a poignant dash—she had no answer to that. Her husband hadn't backed her up.

All Goody Corey was able to say later in her examination, when Hathorne pointed to the afflicted girls, was, "We must not believe distracted persons." She still maintained the girls were not trustworthy. Did anyone listen? No.

The proceeding degenerated into a mob scene. No one seemed to remember or care that this was an examination, not a trial. The accusing girls—and now a few adults, too—rolled around the meetinghouse floor, claiming they'd been bitten. Someone threw her shoe, which hit Goody Corey in the head! The magistrates and constables did absolutely nothing to stop it—and ordered her off to prison in Boston.

Giles rode with his wife as far as the ferry. He didn't have money with him, so he couldn't cross, but he told her he'd join her soon. He'd learn only later his promise was a crushing mistake.

CHAPTER EIGHT

LIKE MOTHER, LIKE DAUGHTER

The Putnams kept spinning their web—and then they caught the littlest fly. Ann started claiming that back on the night of March 3, Goody Good's daughter, Dorothy, had pinched and bitten her. Ann said Dorothy's specter had put her little hands around her neck and almost choked her, and had also tried to get Ann to sign a pact with the Devil.

Dorothy was only about four years old! She was completely vulnerable to the allegations because she was so young. New Englanders carried with them the Old Country belief that family members of witches were more likely to be witches themselves. And family members of an accused person were more likely to be charged themselves, even if the original accusation was decades old and the defendant had been acquitted. Dorothy's young age, combined with the witchcraft charges against her mother, not to mention the fact her mother was in jail and unable to protect her, put her in an extremely dangerous position.

Nothing was done about Ann's allegations against Dorothy while she was the only one complaining, but then Ann's older cousin Mary Walcott complained about Dorothy, too, and two of the Putnam men filed charges. On March 23 a warrant was sworn out for the little girl's arrest. Hathorne mistakenly wrote Dorothy Good's first name as "Dorcas." The authorities didn't always know the first name of female defendants; they were known simply as the "wife" or "daughter" of a man.

Let that sink in. She was four years old and they didn't even know her name—but by golly, they were going to arrest her.

The Putnams were driving the witch hunt on. And if this accusation against a child wasn't stunning enough, just wait until you hear about their next accusation.

"A PALE WOMAN"

Witchcraft allegations had first been made against vulnerable outsiders—the Caribbean slave, Tituba; the ostracized Goody Osborne; the disagreeable mumbler, Goody Good. With the imprisonment of Goody Corey, though, it seemed like the mob could take down almost anyone, and if the accusers wanted to test that, there was no one better to target than Rebecca Nurse. Almost deaf and somewhat ill, Goody Nurse was seventy-one years old and of impeccable reputation. She and her husband were on the Porter side of the Putnam-Porter divide, and they'd gotten wealthy while the Putnams' fortunes had fallen.

Goody Nurse wasn't openly skeptical of the witchcraft allegations like Goody Corey, but she said she thought some of the accused were innocent. That threatened the afflicted girls and their allies, such as Thomas Putnam. If they were accusing *innocent* people, surely their own judgment and motives would be subject to serious questions, and *that* could go badly for them. It was already too late to back down—and they showed no sign of wanting to.

Goody Nurse was a devout church member and as respected as anyone in the community, but one thing in the distant past made her vulnerable. Many years before, someone had accused her mother of witchcraft, but she hadn't been convicted. Now here came Ann Putnam (yes, her again!) to accuse Goody Nurse of attacking her. Goody Nurse was ill in bed when Ann said she was attacked. You think that gave her an alibi? People in Salem thought that even if Goody Nurse's body wasn't up to launching an attack, it didn't mean her specter couldn't do it.

Nobody in Goody Nurse's family believed Ann's accusations. Her son-in-law went to the Putnams to ask if Ann had come up with Rebecca's name herself or if someone had coached her. Ann claimed she'd seen a ghostly image of a pale woman sitting in her grandmother's chair, but she hadn't known who it was, and someone—either her mother or their servant, Mercy; she couldn't recall exactly—had said it sounded like Goody Nurse. Now, in the presence of Nurse's son-in-law, Ann's mother and Mercy pointed the finger at each other, each saying the other one had told Ann the image must be Goody Nurse's specter. Not a very convincing allegation—nobody could quite explain how Nurse was identified. But on March 23, a warrant was sworn charging Rebecca Nurse with witchcraft against Ann and her mother.

"I DO NOT THINK THESE SUFFER AGAINST THEIR WILLS"

Goody Nurse was a sympathetic figure. She had many friends in town, her family believed in her innocence, and she remained extremely poised during her examination on March 24. Perhaps because she had a great deal of credibility—earned over a lifetime—Hathorne began the examination by questioning the afflicted girls: "What do you say? Have you seen this woman hurt you?" Ann immediately replied Nurse had beaten her just that morning. Her mother and Abigail Williams said Nurse had also attacked them. It was only then that Hathorne turned to Nurse and demanded an explanation.

Goody Nurse maintained her innocence—and her composure. She didn't cry, but the crowd counted that against her. Everyone knew witches *couldn't* cry! Honestly, was more proof of witchcraft necessary? Say, are *you* not crying right now? Hmm . . . suspicious.

Nurse tried to deal with the substantive issues and suggested that if her specter appeared to be attacking someone, it wasn't really her—it was the Devil pretending to be her. But it didn't matter. Partway through the proceedings, Mary Walcott and Elizabeth Hubbard decided Nurse had been attacking them, too, and fell into convulsive, thrashing fits.

The afflicted girls started mimicking Nurse. If she leaned in one direction, they flung themselves that way, too, as though she were bewitching them. If she shut her mouth, they claimed they'd been bitten; if she touched her fingertips together, they claimed they were being pinched. When Nurse tilted her head, Elizabeth snapped her head to the same side and Abigail cried out, "Set up Goody Nurse's head! The maid's neck will be broke!" Someone roughly grabbed Goody Nurse's gray-haired head to hold it upright—and sure enough, Elizabeth's head popped back up. Broken neck averted.

Goody Nurse's examination turned into as much of a circus as Goody Corey's had. Ann's mother suddenly went stiff as a board and her husband had to carry her out of the building. There was so much flailing, screaming, and commotion, Reverend Parris noted at the end of his record of the proceedings that he hadn't gotten it all down.

And Nurse was sent to Salem jail. The jail was close enough to a river that water seeped down the walls and it likely had rats. Prisoners accused of being witches were kept not in regular cells but in the dungeon, where it was perpetually dark, damp, and cold in winter, and they were shackled in heavy chains bolted to the walls. That was supposed to make it harder for their specters to escape and cause trouble. On April 12, Goody Nurse was transferred to the prison in Boston.

Ann Putnam had pointed her finger and one of the most respected people in Salem was hauled off in chains.

Twenty-year-old Mary Warren, a servant of John and Elizabeth Proctor, a local couple who ran a tavern and farmed, was another of Rebecca Nurse's accusers. During the examination, Mary had flailed and thrashed with the other afflicted girls. John Proctor was disgusted with his servant's performance. He didn't believe the allegations and thought the accusers were faking their fits, so he threatened to whip Mary if she didn't stop.

Wouldn't you know it? Mary's fits vanished. She went so far as to post a note on the meetinghouse door a few days later confirming her recovery. On Sunday, April 3, Mary told her fellow churchgoers that the "afflicted persons did but dissemble." In other words, the girls were faking it!

Now, why didn't this admission help Rebecca Nurse? Or stop the examinations entirely? I never understood that. It may be because people just don't think clearly when they're afraid. And it was dangerous to try to stop that kind of mass hysteria, because going against a mob could get *you* accused. Goody Corey had been a skeptic and was chained in jail. Goody Nurse told Hathorne, "I do not think these suffer against their wills"—a polite way of saying the afflicted girls were causing their own fits—and now she was in jail, too. And some people saw an advantage in keeping the witch hunt going and benefited from all the fear it was causing. The spider was spinning its web—on the Hanging Tree.

THE LITTLEST WITCH

Dorothy Good was examined on March 24, the same day as Rebecca Nurse. She was said to "cripple with a glance"—just looking at her accusers caused them to suffer physically. Really? A glance from a four-year-old? Several adult men held her small head so she couldn't look at her accusers, but she still managed to glance at the girls and—so they said—afflict them. The men repeated this several times to see if the girls continued to go into fits; they did. No one recorded the effect on a terrified little girl of having her head held by big men's hands so she couldn't move it. Dorothy was jailed in Salem.

On Saturday, March 26, Hathorne and Corwin, accompanied by Salem Town's minister, went to the jail to further interrogate Dorothy. They asked her whether she had a familiar—an animal companion. The little girl supposedly said she had a tiny snake that suckled at the bottom of her index finger. She had a red spot there. It looked like a flea bite, but the men were convinced they'd found a witch's mark! The magistrates asked if the man dressed in black who appeared in other defendants' testimony had given her the little snake and she said no, her mother had.

Maybe she missed her mom and wanted to talk about her. Maybe as a poor kid, she just liked the idea of someone giving her something. But wow, was it the wrong thing to say at the wrong time.

Dorothy remained in jail for a couple of weeks before being transferred to the Boston prison and thrown into the dungeon. She was shackled in heavy chains with tiny manacles. The chains had no lock—only a blacksmith could cut them loose.

She would stay there for eight months.

CHAPTER NINE

CAT SCRATCH FEVER

Reverend Parris gave a sermon on March 27 entitled *Christ Knows How Many Devils There Are in His Churches, and Who They Are.* He began by quoting John 6:70—"Have I not chosen you twelve, and one of you is a Devil?"

As soon as he spoke those words, Rebecca Nurse's sister Sarah Cloyce got up and left, slamming the meetinghouse door behind her. She'd had enough of Reverend Parris's inflammatory sermons about people who pretended to be godly, but secretly worked for the Devil.

Reverend Parris's sermon notes reveal what he said that day:

> *Our Lord Jesus Christ knows how many Devils there are in his Church, & who they are.*
> *There are Devils as well as Saints in Christs Church.*
> *Christ knows how many of these Devils there are.*
> *Christ Knows who these Devils are.*
> *There are Devils as well as Saints in the Church of Christ.*

Goody Cloyce's angry exit drew attention—and put her in the afflicted girls' crosshairs. It took only a week before an official complaint was lodged against Sarah Cloyce. She was accused of attacking Mary Walcott, Ann Putnam, Mercy Lewis, Abigail Williams, and John Indian. All of them! An arrest warrant was issued on April 8.

Sarah Cloyce wasn't accused just because she was angry at Reverend Parris for attacking her sister. (The *minister* says you probably hang out with the Devil? Yeah, that's hard to overcome.) A bitter land dispute had gone on for years between Cloyce and Nurse's father, William Towne, and—you guessed it!—the Putnam clan. A Putnam charging Towne's daughters with a capital crime would be *quite* a way to get revenge for a land dispute, wouldn't it?

Sarah Cloyce and Rebecca Nurse had another sister, Mary Esty. Did she start looking over her shoulder? She should have.

Before Goody Cloyce could have her examination, Sunday services were held on April 10. During the sermon John Indian shouted that Goody Cloyce was biting him! Abigail Williams joined in, yelling Goody Cloyce was attacking her, too. What was going on? Remember John Indian and Abigail lived in Reverend Parris's house and, as an enslaved person and a minor child, were both under his control. Did Reverend Parris engineer a public display to hurt Goody Cloyce's defense as payback for her storming out of church two weeks before? Goody Cloyce slammed the meetinghouse door on Reverend Parris; was he trying to slam the prison door on her?

Sarah Cloyce's examination was held April 11, and this time the proceedings took place in Salem Town, not in Salem Village, because the Salem Town meetinghouse could hold more people and had better light (it had unbroken windows that weren't boarded up). The Deputy

Governor of Massachusetts Bay Colony, Thomas Danforth, oversaw the proceedings, but Hathorne probably asked the questions. Clearly the shocking events in Salem were catching the attention of the wider public, giving the accusers a much bigger platform from which to launch their charges and the witch hunt more momentum.

Reverend Parris kept the record during Goody Cloyce's examination, writing as fast as he could but still resorting to summarizing because it was so loud and chaotic. John Indian said Goody Cloyce had choked him.

"When did I hurt thee?" Cloyce responded directly to John Indian from where she stood at the front of the room. (Why didn't Deputy Governor Danforth prevent the accuser and the accused from arguing back and forth? No one knows.)

John Indian replied, "A great many times."

"Oh! You are a grievous liar," Cloyce retorted.

Then Abigail astonished the gathering by claiming she knew for a fact Goody Cloyce had been a participant at a gathering of forty witches. Forty! This was the kind of outrageous claim sure to keep the authorities hunting for more witches.

Goody Cloyce asked for water, then collapsed onto her seat. She was hauled off to prison in Boston along with her sister and the others. The road took her past the Hanging Tree.

BETTY WASN'T DEAD, BUT THE COW WAS

At the end of March, forty-one-year-old Mary Fuller named Rachel Clinton as a witch. Goody Clinton was a beggar woman in her sixties, impoverished by a marriage late in her life to a man who abandoned her. She lived in Ipswich, a town near Salem that was also in Essex County.

It seems Goody Clinton had shown up at the Fuller house a few mornings before, on March 23 or 24, and, Fuller said, "charged me with raising lies [about her]."

In Fuller's deposition against Goody Clinton, she explained that while Clinton was yelling at her, Fuller's nephew, who had seen their servant Betty collapse just as Goody Clinton was nearing the Fuller house, "came in and said their Betty was fell down dead." It turned out the servant wasn't actually dead, but just remained unconscious for three hours. Either way, what happened to Betty was sure proof, Fuller said, Goody Clinton was a witch.

On Tuesday, March 29, the Essex County Court went into session. It dealt with regular legal concerns, like men playing cards in the watch house while on duty. It also appointed new constables. One of those appointed that day was Joseph Fuller, Mary Fuller's husband. He just got police powers, and what was his first order of business? To arrest Goody Clinton, an order he carried out that very morning. Clinton was told to present herself for examination at eight o'clock on March 30.

At Goody Clinton's examination the next morning, some surprise witnesses testified against her. Forty-eight-year-old Thomas Burnam said he'd noticed one of his cows was sometimes milked before he did the milking in the mornings—someone had gotten to her first. Who was stealing his milk? He decided to get to the bottom of it. "I arose one night a little before day & stood in my Indian corn near where my cows lay & soon I saw a female stand in the middle of the yard where the cows were, which by her attire I thought was Rachel Clinton." Another time, Burnam testified, he saw an unknown person milking one of his cows and that person suddenly shapeshifted into the "likeness of a gray cat & ran up the back side of my house scratching upon the shingles."

The next spring he found the very same cow dead in the field and he was sure Clinton was to blame.

Then thirty-six-year-old William Baker said he'd brewed strong beer on a day Goody Clinton had dropped by, and that she'd become offended by something during their conversation. He later saw her pacing up and down the lane that led to his house, and the next night the woman who checked on his beer found the barrel completely empty! How could that be? Did the barrel leak? Baker tested that idea, filling the barrel with water to see if it leaked—and it didn't! The missing beer, therefore, must have been bewitched away by Rachel Clinton. No chance somebody had a keg party and didn't tell the boss.

Mary and John Edwards, in their early fifties, testified together that one January day Mary was making blood puddings (an English delicacy made with pig's blood) when Goody Clinton stopped by and mentioned how much she loved them. She asked for one and Mary gave her just that—one. Mary said Clinton seemed upset—she must have thought Mary was being stingy—and left, muttering. While Mary didn't catch what she said, apparently it was a curse, because a couple of weeks later five of the Edwardses' eight-week-old piglets took ill and died.

Mary added that she'd overheard her children once ask Goody Clinton why her hands were all scratched up and Clinton had said two or three "roguish cats" had scratched her.

Beer going missing from a barrel, piglets dying in a frigid New England winter, cats scratching their owner. Everyday troubles? Or witchcraft? Such simple, common events became proof that people in Salem Village were besieged by Satan. Without other explanations because they had little understanding of science or medicine—or, apparently, the nature of cats—people could believe that a muttering neighbor had caused their misfortunes. Goody Clinton was chained up in the Ipswich jail.

Rachel Clinton's was the first case that came from outside Salem Village, and it introduced a whole new cast of accusers. Now people beyond Salem Village had reason to tremble in the night.

CHAPTER TEN

A FAMILY UNDER FIRE

That April 8 warrant for Sarah Cloyce also named Elizabeth Proctor, who was pregnant, although she may not have known it at the time, and already the mother of five children and stepmother of six. She was vulnerable to charges of witchcraft because more than twenty years before, her grandmother had been accused of the same charge. Her grandmother hadn't been convicted, but people thought witchcraft ran in families, so there would've been whispers about Goody Proctor. When enough people whisper, it rustles the leaves of the Hanging Tree.

Elizabeth was married to John Proctor—remember him? He thought the girls were faking their fits and said so in public. He also thought the judicial proceedings were unjust. His skepticism tore at the web of accusations, questioning the legitimacy of witchcraft charges and the motivations of the accusers. That rattled the spider in the middle of the web.

If the way to get back at William Towne was to accuse and arrest his daughters, the way to silence John Proctor was to accuse and arrest his wife.

Wouldn't you know it, Ann Putnam was one of Goody Proctor's accusers, and she claimed something striking. She said Goody Proctor's specter attacked her on March 3 (the very same night she said little Dorothy Good choked her), but Ann *hadn't realized who it was* until she saw Goody Proctor in church the following Sunday, March 6. Had she made her accusation, then filled in the witch's name later?

The complaint was filed on Monday, April 4. Elizabeth is identified only as the "wife of John Proctor"—her first name was left blank. By the time her arrest warrant was issued four days later, the constables had learned her name and added it to the documents. You'd think if people were confident enough of your identity to arrest you in a capital crime, they would know your name.

WE FORGOT TO BARK

A chilling incident occurred before Goody Proctor's examination. Several of the afflicted girls were sitting in Ingersoll's Tavern when they heard a man say he'd heard Goody Proctor was going to be interrogated for witchcraft. Ingersoll's wife said she hadn't heard anything about it, and at that instant, one of the girls cried out Goody Proctor was attacking her. And sure enough, the other girls quickly joined in.

The thing was, the girls didn't bother to go into their convulsive fits this time. They shouted about being attacked by Goody Proctor, but that's it. No flopping around. No lolling tongues. No barking. Perhaps they were emboldened by taking down so many witches already that they didn't think they had to have the fits anymore. Or maybe they just forgot?

The man who'd initiated the whole thing said he didn't believe the girls and Goody Ingersoll told them to knock it off. The girls had grown used to adults falling for anything they said—they'd certainly stirred up mob scenes at all the examinations. But now, in this more skeptical atmosphere, they immediately backed off—and one of them said she'd just made the claim against Goody Proctor "for sport." Hold on! Could the girls be accusing people of witchcraft just to break the boredom of life in a Puritan village? Just . . . for *fun*?

The man from the tavern told the court what had happened. Did that discredit the afflicted girls? End the trials? No. It didn't even affect Goody Proctor's trial! Her accusers *clearly* faked their fits, which were the evidence on which the charges rested. And it did absolutely nothing to stop the proceedings against her.

A man named Samuel Barton testified he'd gone to the Putnams to try to help out since their household was in turmoil because of the fits. While there, he'd overheard something troubling: Thomas and his wife urging their servant, Mercy, to say she'd been afflicted by Elizabeth Proctor, and Mercy insisting *she hadn't been*. Despite her denials, the Putnams told Mercy she'd been bitten and pinched by Goody Proctor a few days before and just didn't realize it. It appeared to Barton the Putnams were trying to create a case against Proctor and influence what a witness would say.

And it worked! Mercy would go on to give a statement accusing Goody Proctor of torturing her "by biting and pinching me most grievously," a line she'd apparently been fed by the Putnams. Barton provided a statement about all of this to the court. He told everyone!

But it had no more effect than the testimony about the events at Ingersoll's Tavern.

Goody Proctor was examined right after Goody Cloyce on April 11, with her husband there to support her. Deputy Governor Danforth began the examination by reminding both Proctor and her accusers they should tell the truth because one day they would have to answer before God. He then asked Ann Putnam, Abigail Williams, Mary Walcott, and Mercy Lewis whether Goody Proctor had hurt them. And *they didn't say a word.* Huh—interesting. Perhaps his warning had frightened them?

But then John Indian identified Goody Proctor as the specter that had shown up in her nightgown to choke *him.* As soon as John Indian said Goody Proctor had afflicted him, Ann regained her ability to speak—eureka!—and accused Proctor. Then Ann and Abigail fell into fits, throwing the proceedings into an uproar. At one point, Ann made a fist and tried to punch Goody Proctor, but her fist "magically" opened as she swung so only her fingers brushed Proctor's hood. At this Ann cried out that Goody Proctor was burning her fingers!

The afflicted girls shouted that John Proctor was also performing witchcraft! A husband-and-wife witch team—that was terrifying. And, they said, he was about to make Goody Pope's feet rise into the air. Sure enough, a moment later up went Pope's feet. Then Abigail exclaimed Mary Walcott was about to have a fit—and a moment later Mary went into very impressive convulsions. Two of the accusers were later called "visionary girls" because they could foresee events like the rising of Goody Pope's feet and Mary's fit before they happened. No way would Goody Pope have lifted her feet and Mary faked a fit just to fulfill the predictions. Right?

The girls claimed that while Sarah Cloyce, Rebecca Nurse, Martha Corey, and Sarah Good were chained in jail, their specters were all at a gathering of witches right that very moment! Also, there was Goody Proctor sitting on a ceiling beam above them in the meetinghouse! How could her specter possibly be perched on the ceiling, kicking her heels, if she hadn't flown there?

The crowd was in an uproar!

PLEASE DON'T SIT IN THE JUDGE'S LAP

At the end of Goody Proctor's examination, Ann, Abigail, Mercy, and Mary charged John Proctor with attacking them. He retorted that the girls claiming to be bewitched would wind up accusing everyone in Salem if they weren't careful, and *they* were the ones who should be hanged. Whoa. That was dangerous talk. It's very possible the afflicted girls thought they had no choice but to take down John Proctor or risk being taken down themselves.

Proctor was immediately questioned, and during his examination, Abigail cried out he was sitting in a magistrate's lap. Mary confirmed that, yes, Proctor was sitting in the magistrate's lap. It was a ludicrous charge! Previous defendants had been blamed for pinching, biting, or choking the accusers, but claiming an adult man (or his specter) was sitting in the lap of a judge? That was humiliating. Who was the adult now, and who the lap-sitting child? John Proctor had openly said he thought the girls were lying, and this was his punishment.

Though Proctor was accused and questioned during his wife's examination, no formal charge seems to have been made against him and no arrest warrant was issued. In a shocking breakdown in the legal process, Proctor was sent off to Salem jail anyway, along with his wife and Goody Cloyce.

The next day, April 12, the Proctors, Goody Cloyce, Goody Nurse, and little Dorothy Good were all transferred out of Salem jail, which was getting too crowded. They were sent to Boston, where they were imprisoned with the women sent there earlier and shackled in lockless chains designed to be heavy enough that it was hard to move. At least Dorothy was reunited with her mother and baby sister, though even that was a mixed blessing: Sarah Good's infant daughter died in prison sometime before the middle of July, and Dorothy undoubtedly saw her sister perish.

Not all of Salem's victims were hanged. That's a thing I know for sure.

CHAPTER ELEVEN

HERE A WITCH, THERE A WITCH, EVERYWHERE A WITCH

The Proctors' servant, Mary Warren, hadn't attended Goody Proctor's examination—which turned into John Proctor's examination, too—and Abigail took advantage of her absence. She claimed Goody Proctor's specter told her Mary had signed the Devil's book! Mary hadn't supported the prosecution of her employers, and perhaps that's why Abigail accused her—or maybe it was payback for Mary telling anyone in church who would listen back on April 3 that the girls were faking their fits. On Saturday, April 16, the afflicted girls said Mary's specter attacked them, and the following Monday a warrant was issued for her arrest.

At Mary's examination on April 19, all the girls fell into fits, and so did Goody Pope. A few moments later John Indian joined in, apparently realizing being an accuser was safer than waiting to be accused. After all, Mary had been one of their own and recanted—and now she was paying the price.

Mary refused to name names and was quickly sent to Salem jail; when she was examined again, she fell into such continual and ferocious fits she was unable to talk. It's hard not to see that as Mary's attempt to avoid charging the Proctors, on whom she depended for her living. Eventually she did accuse Goody Proctor, but that wasn't enough, and after three weeks chained to a damp dungeon wall, she agreed to everything her inquisitors wanted, including accusing John Proctor of witchcraft. Mary was effectively taking back her statements that the accusers were faking fits and lying, and she never again tried to turn on the accusers. The web of lies was too strong to escape.

I know that because I saw it all. I was there—and I took part in what happened at Salem.

I CUT YOUR COAT WITH MY SWORD!

By this point, witch hysteria was nearing fever pitch—accusers claimed to see witches' yellow birds flying overhead all the time (and yet somehow, they never pooped on the people below). And arrest warrants against accused witches weren't being issued one at a time, but in groups. The day Mary Warren was examined, Hathorne and Corwin also examined Bridget Bishop, Giles Corey, and Abigail Hobbs.

Goody Bishop was in her early fifties, lived in Salem Town, and was the wife of a sawyer, or lumber cutter. She said, in apparent bewilderment, she'd never even *been* to Salem Village before her deposition and had never seen the girls who were accusing her. This was undoubtedly true. But the girls would have known Goody Bishop by reputation—which wasn't good. Twelve years before, in 1680, Goody Bishop had been accused of witchcraft. An enslaved man claimed she'd frightened horses and stolen eggs, and her specter had pinched him. In what had been a less hysterical environment, she'd been exonerated. But the gossip lingered . . .

In the years since, other people had accused Goody Bishop of causing problems that couldn't be explained. A Salem Town couple lost their eldest child and didn't know the cause of death—so they thought bewitchment by Goody Bishop was the logical answer. Their pain and helplessness were real. It would be terrifying to watch a family member decline and die, be unable to stop it, and not know how or why it had happened; you'd want someone to blame. The small seeds of suspicion gossip planted years before had grown into a briar patch of fear.

At Goody Bishop's examination the accusers mimicked her, just as they had other defendants previously. She moved her head, her hands, or her eyes; the girls moved their heads, hands, or eyes in the same way—a horrific, twisted game of copycat. And Bishop couldn't do a thing about it.

At an earlier examination, Mary Walcott saw a specter in a white sheet, which her father grabbed at as it flew past. Her father's hand jerked, and he opened his fist to show the crowd the piece of ripped sheet. Aha! Proof a specter was there among them! Apparently, it occurred to no one that he could have walked in with a piece of sheet hidden away for a reveal at the appropriate time.

Having gotten away with that, Mary tried a similar trick at Goody Bishop's examination. She shouted that her brother, Jonathan, had whacked Bishop's specter with his sword! He'd torn Bishop's coat—Mary heard it rip. The magistrates examined Goody Bishop's coat and found that it was indeed ripped. Proof of the claim against Goody Bishop!

But wait . . . there was a problem. It wasn't a clean cut like a sword would make. It looked much more like someone had come up behind her and ripped her coat by hand. And that wouldn't be proof of witchcraft, but of fraud. Mary quickly said Jonathan hadn't unsheathed the sword, but swung it in the scabbard, and so the tear looked exactly as it should. This was straight-up deception! (Also, who swings a sword without bothering to take it out of the scabbard? That's just weird.) It's hard to imagine why anyone fell for that. Would *you* have? And yet Goody Bishop was thrown in Salem jail.

"I HAVE BEEN VERY WICKED"

You remember Giles Corey, who testified against his wife, Martha, on March 21? Well, Corey had a long history of bad behavior. He'd once thrown water on the schoolmaster, which led to a fistfight. In a period of wars with Indigenous people, when colonists were terrified and the danger of a raid was real, when it was his turn to stand watch, Corey had abandoned his post to fetch a load of wood—and then lied about it in court. Worst of all, he'd once beaten a servant who was stealing from him so severely that the man died of his injuries and Corey had been punished for his death.

Ironically, Corey, who hadn't supported his wife at her examination, ended up being hurt by a show of devotion to her. The day Goody Corey was sent to the Boston prison, he'd traveled alongside her the fifteen miles overland to the ferry but then said he'd join her later. Some people who overheard him were convinced he was admitting to witchcraft—and accused him.

So on April 19, here was Giles Corey being examined by Hathorne, who asked, "Did you not say, when you went to the ferry with your wife, you would not go over to Boston now, for you should come yourself next week?" Corey explained that he did not have the fare to cross, but Hathorne suggested he was assuring his wife he was a witch and would soon be imprisoned with her.

Now Hathorne ordered one of Corey's hands to be untied. This was a test. And sure enough, whatever physical movements Corey made, the afflicted girls made the very same movements. He tilted his head sideways; their heads snapped to the side. He sucked in his cheeks; their cheeks sucked in, too. Here was proof Corey's specter was controlling the girls! Hathorne ordered Corey off to jail—because he'd lost a game of mirrors.

Fourteen-year-old Abigail Hobbs was also examined on April 19, but hers was a very different case from that of Goody Bishop or Giles Corey. The Hobbs family were refugees from wars with Indigenous nations in Maine and lived in Topsfield, near Salem. Abigail's father hadn't been to church in a long time, which was scandalous, and Abigail herself was known as an ungovernable "free spirit." That was a very bad thing to be in seventeenth-century Massachusetts Bay Colony! Abigail slept in the woods under the stars and was well known for speaking irreverently and expressing no fear of the Devil. Ann Putnam had been the first to accuse her; several of the other girls jumped in and lodged accusations of their own.

When confronted with the charges, Abigail confessed! Maybe she didn't try to defend herself because she knew that if a pillar of the community like Goody Nurse could be convicted, she had no hope of denying the accusations. "I have seen sights and been scared. I have been very wicked. I hope I shall be better; if God will keep me." None of the usual accusers went into fits at her examination, and they even expressed some sorrow for her afterward. But if the accusers were having remorse, it didn't last long.

Abigail Hobbs's confession rocked Salem Village, much as Tituba's had before her. While charges had been lodged against ten people, no one else had admitted to witchcraft except Dorothy Good, who was too little to know any better. The accusers had claimed several times to know about large gatherings of witches, but if that was true, where were all those witches? Now, finally, someone else who was old enough to testify had confessed.

Goody Bishop, Giles Corey, and Abigail Hobbs were chained in the dungeon in Salem jail. They were joined over the next seven weeks by *fifty-four* more people accused of witchcraft, including many who lived outside of Salem Village—likely to be people who, like Abigail Hobbs, the accusers may never have known.

The Devil was walking even faster through the streets of Salem.

So here's a thing, and it's important: How did the afflicted girls know who Hobbs was? If they'd never seen the person they were accusing of pinching and choking them, how did they know it was *that* person's specter? The girls' answer was always the same: *The specter had told the girls their name.* Seriously? Why would witches identify themselves by name when it would lead to their death? That was never answered. It was never even asked.

CHEATING ON A TEST

Eight people were examined on Friday, April 22. Twenty-seven-year-old weaver Nehemiah Abbott Jr. was *let go*, the only person in all of the Salem witch hunt to be exonerated immediately. How did Abbott cheat the Hanging Tree? He maintained his innocence with unusual confidence. His self-assurance caused Hathorne, who'd questioned the girls about their identification of witches they'd never met, to now tell the girls not to accuse Abbott if it wasn't his specter that had appeared to them.

Under Hathorne's questioning, some of the girls admitted they weren't sure, and because of the crushing crowd, they couldn't get a good look at Abbott. So Hathorne and Corwin moved the proceedings outside. Interestingly, the examination didn't have the same energy outside—people weren't packed together, feeding off one another's excitement or hysteria. Now, face-to-face with the man they'd accused of a capital crime, the girls apparently lost their nerve. They announced Abbott looked *just like* the specter that had tormented them—except Abbott didn't have a wart on his nose. And for that reason—and that reason alone—Abbott was let go.

The April 21 warrant also charged Mary Black, an African woman enslaved by Nathaniel Putnam, Thomas Putnam's uncle. She certainly fit into the category of a powerless outsider. She maintained her innocence but was clearly nervous during her examination. Who wouldn't be? When Black fiddled with the fabric at her neck, Hathorne asked if she was doing something satanic.

"No, I pin my neckcloth," Black replied.

Hathorne told her to do it again. And wouldn't you know it? As soon as she shoved the pin through her neckcloth, the afflicted girls howled. Mary Black was sent to Salem jail, then transferred to Boston on May 13.

Mary Esty was the sister of Rebecca Nurse and Sarah Cloyce, the only daughter of Putnam's old nemesis William Towne, who hadn't been accused—until now. During her examination the afflicted girls were unable to speak because their fits were so severe. Goody Esty maintained her innocence, but as soon as she clasped her hands together, Mercy's hands smacked together so hard she was unable to separate them until a constable made Esty unclasp her hands, which "freed" Mercy's, too. Predictably, Ann Putnam was the first to regain the ability to speak—and accused Mary Esty. The girls went on to claim Goody Esty had tried to get them all to sign the Devil's book. She was sent to Salem jail.

YOUR SCARF
OFFENDS US

As the girls began to accuse people they'd never met but had overheard adults talk about, how could the magistrates be sure the girls were identifying them accurately? Well, Hathorne and Corwin devised a test for the girls. When Deliverance Hobbs, Abigail's mother, was brought into the meetinghouse for her examination on April 22, her name wasn't announced. Hathorne asked two of the afflicted girls if they knew her, and both were unable to answer, even though *they claimed her specter had attacked them.* Ann eventually named her after an older relative whispered in her ear, apparently giving her Goody Hobbs's name! Does your teacher allow *you* to answer a test question this way—by having someone whisper the answer to you? Probably better not find out.

With her accusers shrieking and rolling around, Goody Hobbs confessed to everything the magistrates suggested. We don't know why. She may have just caved under pressure, or maybe she'd realized that as long as Salem couldn't hold trials, a confession didn't lead to execution, but did end the humiliation of a witchcraft examination. Perhaps she was just following the lead of her daughter, Abigail, who'd stunned the crowd with her confession.

But then Goody Hobbs dropped her own bombshell: There was a witches' church in town, she said, complete with a preacher who served communion with red bread and red wine. Goody Hobbs said the witches' minister had told them to bewitch everyone in Salem, one by one. And—drumroll—the minister was Reverend George Burroughs, Salem Village's former pastor! It seems a Puritan's imagination couldn't contemplate a society that didn't revolve around the church, even if it was made up of witches!

The accused Goody Hobbs then in turn accused Sarah Wilds, a woman in her mid-sixties who was one of the people already being examined that day. Goody Wilds had a bit of a reputation, having been reprimanded years before for wearing a silk scarf, which was too fancy for Puritan Salem. Whether Hathorne was overwhelmed with the number of people being questioned that day or he was convinced by Hobbs's accusations against Wilds, she seems to have had a quicker examination than usual. When the afflicted girls claimed to see Wilds sitting on a ceiling beam, she had little chance to say anything to defend herself.

With his wife and daughter now having confessed to witchcraft, William Hobbs was in a precarious position. In *his* examination, he made a solid effort to defend himself, but Abigail shouted that his specter was about to attack Mercy, and—on cue—Mercy fell into a fit. Then Abigail shouted that Hobbs's specter was coming for Mary, and—on cue—Mary fell into a fit.

Hathorne asked Hobbs whether he wanted to confess as his wife had, and Hobbs replied he was not a witch and hurt no one.

"When were you at any public religious meeting?" Hathorne asked.

"Not a pretty while." Hobbs was admitting he hadn't attended church in a long time.

"Why so?"

"Because I was not well; I had a distemper that none knows." By saying he'd been sick, but no one knew about it, Hobbs may have been attempting to keep the crowd from testifying he'd been well enough to go to church, but just didn't want to.

Hathorne took more digs at Hobbs, but Hobbs never wavered in maintaining his innocence. He was sent to jail.

CHAPTER TWELVE

LIAR, LIAR, SHUFFLEBOARD ON FIRE

The parade of defendants seemed endless—and there was still no possibility of trying them, because Massachusetts Bay Colony still didn't have a new charter. The conditions in Salem jail, always unpleasant, would have been appalling as the weather got warmer. And its smelly, bedraggled suspects had to pay for their own chains—and for having them put on.

An April 21 arrest warrant naming nine people included Bridget Bishop's stepson, Edward, and his wife, Sarah, who were examined on April 22. It's likely they were both accused because of what Puritans considered scandalous behavior— they ran a tavern where people could play shuffleboard, a game where the players slid discs into a scoring area. Shocking! Puritans opposed the playing of any games—games distracted people from God and led to all sorts of trouble. (It wasn't until around the time of the American Revolution, nearly eighty-five years after the Salem witch trials, that

playing ball sports started being socially acceptable.) On top of that, people complained the tavern's customers tended to be too loud, and too drunk, and to stay up too late.

The shuffleboard games upset one local woman so much she stomped into the Bishops' tavern, grabbed the shuffleboard pieces, and flung them into the fire. The same woman later killed herself by cutting her own throat with a pair of scissors! People didn't want to believe she'd done that to herself; it was too horrifying, and easier to believe she'd been bewitched. People recalled that tragedy once witchcraft allegations started flying in Salem, and they gave Sarah Bishop the squint eye—and accused her of witchcraft.

Her husband, Edward, was also accused, not just because he was a relative of accused witch Goody Bishop and his newly accused wife, but because people knew he didn't believe the witchcraft allegations. The night of April 11, after the Proctors' examinations, Edward Bishop gave John Indian a ride home on his horse. John Indian had a fit while sitting behind Bishop and bit him, then held on with his teeth. Bishop wasn't having that! He hit John Indian with a stick and told him to cut it out, and his fit stopped. Not only that, but John Indian promised not to have another one—almost as though they were voluntary. Bishop muttered he could end the accusations completely if he could whack *all* the accusers with a stick, and many other people on the road heard him. As soon as Bishop turned off to go to his own house, the girls began to cry out he was tormenting them. Cowards! They wouldn't say it to his face.

Bishop's ability to stop John Indian's fit made the fits look awfully suspicious—and that was dangerous to the afflicted girls. There was no easy way for the people making accusations to stop and keep their credibility, so they absolutely had to keep Salem Village believing them.

And that meant they had to silence people who said they were liars—as John Proctor had, and Mary Warren, and now Edward Bishop.

Mary English was the last person listed on that arrest warrant of April 21. She was accused by Ann Putnam, Mercy Lewis, and Mary Walcott in a complaint sworn by Thomas Putnam, and she was examined on April 22.

Goody English was the wife of Salem Town's wealthiest merchant, Philip English, who'd been born on an island off the coast of France and spoke with an accent. He had a large shop and traded all sorts of goods not just with England and the West Indies, but also with France, Spain, and Portugal—the first New Englander to do so. By 1692 he owned more than twenty ships and a large house. English's extraordinary success and vague Frenchness set him apart.

In addition, English had been elected in March to political office in Salem Town—a post the Putnams had been coveting for themselves. So it was no surprise at all that Thomas Putnam swore out the complaint charging Mary English with witchcraft.

Unfortunately, examination records for Edward Bishop, Sarah Bishop, and Mary English don't survive, so we can't know exactly what they said to defend themselves. But we know this: Edward Bishop said he was innocent. Sarah Bishop said she was innocent. Mary English said she was innocent. All three were sent to jail and transferred to Boston on May 13 to await trial.

LIARS

Three more accused witches were thrown in jail based on a mass complaint sworn by Thomas Putnam on April 30.

Dorcas Hoar and Susannah Martin, both of whom were skeptical the girls were bewitched, maintained their innocence during their examinations on May 2. Dorcas Hoar, from the town of Beverly, called the girls "liars," and Hathorne told her she couldn't say that in court. Goody Hoar had a terrible reputation. She was a widow who practiced palm reading and fortune-telling, although apparently only unpleasant fortunes, like telling people when they'd die. She also had a significant blemish on her record—she'd once helped her own minister's servant steal from his family. Folks in and around Salem had known about her palm reading for years, but hadn't thought much about it until witchcraft allegations began to fly in early 1692. Goody Hoar's interest in predicting the future doomed her, and she was sent to Salem jail.

Susannah Martin was a diminutive seventy-one-year-old from the town of Amesbury who'd once challenged her seat in the meetinghouse. Seats were assigned by rank, and Goody Martin apparently wanted a better one. She'd been accused of witchcraft years earlier. Her husband, a blacksmith, had sued the accusers for slander and won. But now she was widowed and therefore more vulnerable.

Goody Martin laughed when Ann Putnam threw a glove at her at the beginning of her examination on May 2. Shocked, Hathorne asked, "What do you laugh at it?"

"Well I may at such folly," Martin replied, openly contemptuous of the girls' allegations.

"Is this folly? The hurt of these persons?"

Martin backtracked then, saying, "I never hurt man woman or child."

The afflicted girls shouted that Susannah Martin had hurt them many times, and Martin could only reply, "I have no hand in witchcraft."

Hathorne pressed her. "Do not you think they are bewitched?"

"No, I do not think they are."

Uh-oh! Thinking the afflicted girls were faking fakers didn't usually turn out well.

Later in the examination, Hathorne came back to that. "Do you believe these do not say true?"—meaning did she think the girls were lying.

"They may lie for ought I know."

"May not you lie?" Hathorne shot back.

When Martin bit her lip in frustration, the afflicted girls, including John Indian, screamed she was biting them. It was impossible for Susannah Martin to prove herself innocent since the magistrates accepted spectral evidence, and she was sent to jail.

Like Goody Martin and Goody Hoar, Lydia Dustin was also a widow. She'd long been suspected of witchcraft. A decade before, one of her neighbors had gotten drunk, thrown rocks at Dustin's daughter's house, and declared Lydia Dustin was a witch. It had given her a poor reputation. (I always thought it should have given the rock-throwing drunk a poor reputation.) Now, at age eighty, Goody Dustin was arrested along with two of her daughters and a granddaughter. The record of her examination doesn't survive.

Philip English, the wealthy merchant with the coveted political office and husband of the recently interrogated Mary English, was included in Putnam's April 30 complaint. But when the warrant was issued and the constables came for him, he wasn't anywhere to be found. Philip English had fled. Wouldn't you?

CHAPTER THIRTEEN

ACCUSATIONS, AFFLICTIONS, AND ARRESTS

The first name listed on Thomas Putnam's April 30 complaint was one of the biggest of the Salem witch hunt: Reverend George Burroughs, Salem's former minister. Ann Putnam claimed she had a hallucination in which Reverend Burroughs's two deceased wives told her he'd murdered them! A warrant was issued for his arrest the same day as Putnam's complaint, and a marshal and soldiers were sent north to Maine to arrest him and transport him back to Salem. He finally arrived on May 4.

Reverend Burroughs had had a hard time since he'd left Salem. He'd been in the most far-flung British settlement way up north and was the only minister in the region, which was near some heavy fighting between French colonists with their Indigenous allies and the English colonists. His second wife died, leaving him with seven children, and he moved his family to Wells, Maine. In 1692, a nearby community was wiped out in the fighting and refugees had flooded into Wells, which was itself in constant danger of attack. When a company of soldiers arrived in town, people thought they were the reinforcements they'd been begging for. They weren't. They'd come from Salem to arrest the minister!

At Reverend Burroughs's examination on May 9, the afflicted girls fell into their usual terrible fits. People testified against the minister, saying he'd treated his second wife badly. That may have been true but wasn't proof of witchcraft. Reverend Burroughs *had* lost two wives, but he vigorously denied he'd murdered them. Reverend Burroughs did admit under questioning, however, that his house in Maine had toads— which were creatures associated with the Devil. Do *you* have a toad in your house? In a fish tank, maybe? Better be careful . . .

Then a number of witnesses, including men who'd fought alongside him in the Indigenous wars in Maine, spoke of his remarkable physical strength. It wasn't a compliment. Reverend Burroughs wasn't a big guy and the men were suggesting it was only through a pact with the Devil that Burroughs had such strength, which he'd undoubtedly been granted in return for doing evil deeds. The astonished minister was hauled off to the Boston prison.

George Jacobs Sr. and his seventeen-year-old granddaughter, Margaret Jacobs, were also accused. The elderly Jacobs, who needed two canes to walk, maintained his innocence at his examination on May 10. When Hathorne began to read the names of Jacobs's accusers, he'd only gotten through "Abigail Williams" when, the record reports, "Jacobs laughed." Asked why he was laughing, Jacobs said, "Because I am falsely accused . . . I never did it."

Hathorne asked, "Who did it?"

"Don't ask me," Jacobs retorted.

George Jacobs's live-in servant, Sarah Churchill, was one of his accusers. She was another refugee from the wars in Maine and had seen both of her parents murdered. In the chaos, Sarah shouted directly at Jacobs: "You had as good confess if you are guilty."

"Have you heard that I have any witchcraft?" Jacobs replied.

"I know you lived a wicked life." Sarah was about twenty years old; Jacobs was eighty. She was taking a huge risk sassing her elder—not to mention her employer—in this way. But the examinations were blowing all the rules out of the water. And maybe, for the accusers, that was their charm.

Sarah also complained that when she couldn't do her chores because she'd had a fit like the afflicted girls, Jacobs had called her a nasty name: "bitch witch."

Hathorne asked Sarah if George Jacobs ever prayed. She said he didn't unless he did so alone, in which case she wouldn't witness it. When Hathorne asked Jacobs why he didn't pray, Jacobs replied, "I cannot read."

Hathorne demanded Jacobs recite the Lord's Prayer, which was a prayer everybody had memorized, so it wouldn't matter that he couldn't read. It was also a great test—a witch couldn't recite the Lord's Prayer without making a mistake (or so it was believed). Of course, under the extreme pressure of being interrogated for witchcraft, it would be extremely hard for anyone to recite it perfectly, witch or not. The elderly man stumbled over the lines several times and at the end of his examination, he blustered, "Well! Burn me or hang me, I will stand in the truth of Christ, I know nothing of it."

At one point during Jacobs's examination, Ann and Abigail showed off their hands. Each had a pin stuck in it and they blamed "this old

Jacobs" for pricking them. Hold on a minute! Some testimony can only be taken as deliberate fraud. Those pins didn't get there on their own.

Sarah Churchill was in tears after Jacobs's examination and she told Sarah Ingersoll, the niece of the tavern owners, that she hadn't told the truth. She said Hathorne and Corwin threatened to chain her up in the Salem jail dungeon, so she'd turned on Jacobs to save herself. So . . . threats against a witness resulted in false testimony? Who could have predicted that? Sarah Ingersoll offered testimony of the encounter, cosigned by another woman who overheard it, saying Churchill "came to me crying and wringing her hands." It made no difference.

Something else happened on Tuesday, May 10—something terrible. The witch craze claimed its first fatality: Goody Sarah Osborne died in the Boston prison.

Goody Osborne had been ill when she was arrested in March and had spent nine weeks and two days weighed down by chains designed to be so heavy that movement was difficult. Someone had indeed died because of witchcraft, but it wasn't one of the girls claiming they were afflicted by witches. *Who was the criminal now? Who was the victim?*

On May 11 the constables told George Jacobs Sr.'s granddaughter, Margaret, that if she confessed, she would not be hanged, and if she refused, she would be. Terrified, she confessed, and was sent to Salem jail.

On May 12, Mary Warren gave testimony against Alice Parker. Goody Parker was a sailor's wife, and Mary accused her of sinking a ship and killing its crew through witchcraft. Mary also said her father had promised to mow some grass for Goody Parker, but when he didn't do it, Mary's sister and mother both fell ill, and the beloved mother died. What else could have caused such a tragedy but retaliation by Parker?

(Over some unmown grass?) It was reported that during Goody Parker's examination, Mary had such a bad fit that her tongue, protruding from her mouth, turned black!

Mary recovered from *that* incident well enough to then speak against Ann Pudeator, a wealthy seventy-year-old widow. The record of Goody Pudeator's examination doesn't survive, but we know Mary said Goody Pudeator's specter told her Pudeator had poisoned her own husband and almost killed another man by tossing him out of a cherry tree onto his head!

I know something about trees and about people falling from them, but I've never seen someone fall because of witchcraft—except to be executed with a noose around their neck.

Mary Warren was not just an accuser; she also became one of the accused. She gave testimony on May 12 and was then interrogated herself the same day! Hathorne started her examination with the question of whether Warren knew it was the Devil's book that she signed. She replied, "I did not know it then but I know it now." She deflected by naming other people who were witches, including sisters Rebecca Nurse and Sarah Cloyce, and Sarah Good and her little daughter, Dorothy, all of whom were already in jail awaiting their trials.

On May 13 Margaret Jacobs recanted her confession. She announced she'd lied! In jail, Reverend Burroughs had explained to her that her grandfather would hang, and the reality of this seems to have set in. Margaret taking back her testimony didn't impress the magistrates, though. Instead of accepting it at face value—that during the examination she'd been terrified and had told them what they wanted to hear—they decided she was relapsing into witchcraft and made her

conditions in prison harsher, not allowing her to go out into the prison yard.

Margaret recanting did nothing to help her family, either. The Jacobs family was one of many that had multiple members accused. On May 15, a few days after George Sr.'s and Margaret's examinations, Constable Jonathan Putnam came looking for Margaret's father, George Jr., and her uncle Daniel Andrews, a prominent leader of the anti-Putnam faction. Neither man could be found. It seems, like Philip English, they'd fled. Margaret's mother, Rebecca Jacobs, who'd been mentally unstable for years, was left at home with four children, including a two-year-old. Constable Putnam arrested her, and to get her to go with him, he promised she'd be allowed to return home shortly. But he was lying—he took her off to Salem jail while her children ran after her, crying. Who exactly was doing the Devil's work?

The jails continued to fill. Over the next two months, Thomas Putnam and his allies would accuse dozens more people of being witches. They made twenty complaints, most listing several alleged witches at one time. Over the course of the witchcraft hysteria, Putnam would make more than one hundred twenty charges. Almost one in three defendants was accused by Putnam, and he testified personally against seventeen suspects.

Enough people were now in jail to disrupt the functioning of society. It was expensive to pay for a relative's jail fees—the charges for their upkeep were two shillings, sixpence per week, or about $150 per month today. That was as much as a woman could have earned in a week if she'd been working and not imprisoned. If the accused were in prison in another town, people incurred expenses to visit them.

A significant number of families had lost a family member's labor while they were in prison. Keeping up with farmwork and getting regular meals on the table was increasingly difficult. And dozens of children, many very young, had been left without mothers or fathers, which put huge strains on other families to look out for them and feed them. Salem Village was reeling. The circle of accused people was getting bigger, but their absence was felt in an even wider circle. And in the midst of the untilled fields stood the Hanging Tree, waiting while Thomas Putnam spun his web ever wider.

TURNING THE CORPSE

I'll give you one guess who accused Ann Putnam's neighbor, John Willard, of witchcraft. Did you say Ann Putnam? Bingo! Willard was another one who didn't believe the afflicted girls. He was a Salem constable who *refused to make more witchcraft arrests*—and said he thought *the girls* should hang. When Willard heard Ann was saying he was afflicting her, he visited the Putnams to try to reason with her. That didn't work, and in spectacular fashion, Ann screamed he was torturing her right at that moment, even though he was just standing there, dumbfounded.

Ann claimed Willard appeared spectrally to her and confessed to murdering more than a dozen people. That caused townsfolk to squint at him and rethink all their previous interactions. The Putnams finally accused Willard, and the May 10 warrant for his arrest ended with the charge to the arresting officer, "You are not to fail." But fail he did. Constable John Putnam Jr. went to Willard's house, but Willard had fled.

About a week after the warrant for his arrest was issued, Willard was accused of killing a young man. Early in May, seventeen-year-old

Daniel Wilkins said he'd heard rumors that Willard beat his wife and declared Willard should hang. A few days later Daniel got sick. The doctor thought the cause of the illness was witchcraft and called in Ann, Mercy, and Mary as "experts" in witchcraft to confirm his diagnosis. The girls were all too eager to concur, saying they could see Willard's specter at the sick boy's bedside. Daniel Wilkins died on the night of May 16. Reverend Parris recorded his death as "bewitched to death," and on May 17 a coroner's jury noted that "turning the corpse the blood run out of his nose or mouth or both . . . To the best of our judgements we cannot but think that he died an unnatural death by some cruel hands of witchcraft or diabolical art." The coroner's report was signed by twelve men of Salem Village, three of whom were Putnams, and sent on to Hathorne and Corwin.

John Willard should have been more frightened and he should have run farther. He was found forty miles from Salem and dragged back to be interrogated. As Willard was led into the meetinghouse for his examination on May 18, the afflicted girls fell "in most miserable fits," according to Reverend Parris, who wrote the report for this examination. Hathorne began by saying that running away "is an acknowledgement of guilt, but yet notwithstanding this we require you to confess in this matter." Willard said he'd run because he feared the witchcraft accusation against him.

Willard's examination, like that of other defendants, mixed spectral accusations with mundane village gossip, none of which was, or could be, proven. But his was a short examination. His flight convinced the magistrates of his guilt; were they also disgusted by a constable who'd turned his back on his duty to arrest witchcraft suspects? Willard was accused of beating his wife; he asked them to call his wife to the stand to testify, but they didn't. Then one of the afflicted girls said the Devil was whispering in his ear and "that the dead those that he had murdered were now about him."

"Can you pray the Lord's Prayer?" Hathorne asked.

"Yes," Willard said, but when he tried, he stumbled over the words. He said he was nervous—"It is a strange thing, I can say it at another time"—and laughed, but stumbled again when he attempted it once more. Surely in league with the Devil, John Willard was sent to the Boston prison.

Also on May 18, a warrant was issued for the arrest of Roger Toothaker. In a deposition against him, thirty-six-year-old Thomas Gage said Toothaker had bragged about having taught his daughter how to kill a witch. Toothaker had advised his daughter, Martha, to put an earthen pot of an afflicted person's urine in the oven overnight (sounds eerily like that witch cake, doesn't it?) so that by morning the witch causing the affliction would be dead. But how would Toothaker know how to kill a witch if he wasn't a witch himself? Gage concluded his testimony against Toothaker, saying the man had committed other "things I have forgotten and further sayeth not." Gage knew more about Toothaker but just chose not to tell the court? *Really?* It's astonishing such vague testimony would be allowed in a capital case! Roger Toothaker was sent to prison in Boston on May 20.

Toothaker talked a lot about witches and seems like an obvious person to accuse, but there were also dozens of people—like Thomas Farrar—who were caught in the web of lies and accusations for reasons that leave us scratching our heads. Farrar was accused of witchcraft by Ann Putnam. He was a seventy-five-year-old farmer with a drinking problem that sometimes got him banned from taking communion at church. Once after he'd fallen asleep at a neighbor's, he woke up and wandered into a corner behind an open door, thought he was in the outhouse—and relieved himself. In her deposition Ann got in a particularly rude dig about Farrar, testifying, "There appeared to me the apparition of an old grayhead man with a great nose which tortured me and almost choked me." Was Farrar arrested for witchcraft because he had a big nose and accidentally peed behind someone's door? Was Ann that bored? Or that cruel?

Nathaniel Cary, a shipbuilder from Charlestown, near Boston, started hearing rumors his wife, Elizabeth, was being accused of witchcraft. The person doing the accusing was no one they knew: some young girl all the way over in Salem named Abigail Williams. The Carys traveled to Salem to attend an examination on May 23, assuming they'd be able to persuade the magistrates there was some misunderstanding and that Elizabeth's was a case of mistaken identity. They were about to make a terrible mistake.

They made the half-day voyage to Salem and Nathaniel Cary spoke with Hathorne and Corwin, then snagged a good spot in the meetinghouse and watched in horrified fascination as accused prisoners stood at the front and the afflicted girls twisted about. Cary was disgusted by the whole spectacle. Several times the girls walked over to Elizabeth Cary and asked her name. Oh, that wasn't good. She seems not to have told them, though.

Cary asked his long-time acquaintance Reverend John Hale to arrange a meeting with Abigail Williams. Reverend Parris would only allow the meeting at Ingersoll's Tavern, so the Carys waited there, drinking cider, until Abigail or someone in authority could come talk to them and they could straighten it all out.

Instead, after a short wait, the afflicted girls burst into the tavern and fell into fits—naming Elizabeth Cary as their persecutor! Hathorne and Corwin sent over a warrant for Elizabeth to appear before them. The magistrates were waiting for the Carys at the meetinghouse. Clearly they knew the girls were going to the tavern to have their fits. The Carys had been set up! Were the magistrates *in on it*? Had they told the girls Elizabeth Cary's name? Or had Reverend Parris? Either way, it was a betrayal. The Carys had come to Salem in good faith—but while they waited, unaware, the spiders spun their web.

Goody Cary was required to stand with her arms outstretched during her examination to prevent her from doing any mischief to the girls. When she cried, her husband wiped her tears away. He asked to hold her hand to comfort her, but Hathorne wouldn't let him.

The afflicted girls went into more shrieking convulsions during the examination, and John Indian was brought in. He'd been the man serving the Carys cider at the tavern! He didn't say anything, but "fell down and tumbled about like a hog," as Nathaniel Cary wrote later about the whole incident. The afflicted girls assured Hathorne and Corwin it was Goody Cary causing John Indian's fit, as well as their own. Goody Cary was sent to Salem jail, where she was chained and, Nathaniel reported, started to have convulsions—not a fit caused by some unseen witch, but an actual medical crisis. She didn't get help, but she survived and remained chained in the dungeon.

Nathaniel Cary was horrified at what he had seen, and he attempted to get a change of venue so his wife could be tried somewhere other than Salem. He didn't think she'd get a fair trial there, and, boy, was he right about that! His request was denied.

CHAPTER FOURTEEN

DOG GONE

On May 14 Reverend Increase Mather finally returned from England—with a new charter for Massachusetts Bay Colony! The charter enabled the colony's judicial system to get up and running once more, which meant all those imprisoned people accused of witchcraft could finally get their day in court.

Reverend Mather also brought back a new governor for the colony, appointed by the crown: William Phips. Phips had a military background and expected he'd be focusing his attention on relations with Indigenous people since he was well acquainted with the Wabanaki nations, with whom the English settlers were engaged in bitter fighting. Instead, Phips found the local jails overflowing with supposed witches.

Because he knew it would take weeks, or even months, to set up a court system under the new charter, and because the jails were so overcrowded, on May 27 Governor Phips established a Court of Oyer and Terminer. (*Oyer* means "to hear"; *terminer* means "to find out.") In England, courts of Oyer and Terminer were temporary courts set up to deal with urgent disorders. The governor's order was short and, notably, said nothing about witchcraft: "Upon consideration that there are many criminal offenders now in custody, some whereof have lain long and many inconveniences attending the thronging of the jails at this hot time of the year, there being no judicatories or courts of justice yet established. Ordered: That a Special Commission of Oyer and Terminer be made . . ."

Phips appointed his new deputy governor, William Stoughton, to be the chief judge. Stoughton was widely respected and considered supremely competent, having graduated from Harvard College and gotten a master's degree at Oxford University in England. Once the trials got underway, he'd be the one to sum up the evidence and give a jury its instructions, which could greatly influence the verdicts. He might not have looked so good if you were a defendant, though. He'd been on the court in Boston that had condemned Irish Catholic widow Goody Ann Glover to death for bewitching the Goodwin children back in 1688—and he trusted spectral evidence.

Stoughton would be aided by six associate judges, all magistrates and members of a judicial council set up by the new charter. Now lives were genuinely on the line. Not at some vague point in the future—*now*.

The Salem witch trials were to begin in less than a week.

TRICKY TESTS

At the time Elizabeth Cary was examined, the accusers were at the height of their power, able to destroy their neighbors' lives with just a casual word. The charges were coming so fast it was hard to keep up.

On May 28—the day after the new court was established—a complaint accused *eleven* new witches. The warrant was sworn on behalf of Mary Walcott, Abigail Williams, Mercy Lewis, Ann Putnam, and "others belonging to Salem Village or farms." What a ridiculously sloppy accusation for a capital crime!

One of the eleven, Captain John Floyd, had fought in the wars up in Maine, but was widely considered an incompetent commander. His men had once mutinied during a battle and four Salem men had died under his command, including Susannah Sheldon's older brother. Susannah was one of Floyd's accusers. That sure looks like a clear case of payback, don't you think?

Two of the accused were Mary Toothaker, whose husband, Roger, was already imprisoned in Boston, and their nine-year-old daughter, Margaret.

John Alden, a sailor from Boston, was also accused. Alden's father had arrived in New England on the *Mayflower* and cofounded Plymouth Colony. John Alden was wealthy and respected, and he had just returned from a diplomatic mission to Canada negotiating the release of captives taken by Indigenous warriors. When Alden was examined, one of the afflicted girls who'd been asked to identify him pointed to someone *other* than Alden—but then she finally identified him after a man, possibly Thomas Putnam, whispered to her which man he was.

Alden was such a respected person—and his identification was so obviously suspect—the magistrates sent Alden and the girls out of the dark meetinghouse so they could view him better. In the daylight, the girls formed a ring around Alden and began to taunt him, Ann declaring he'd had children with Indigenous women, something that would've been quite scandalous. Back inside the meetinghouse, as soon as Alden looked at the girls, they all fell down, their usual tactic to "prove" he was attacking them. Alden had the nerve to ask one of the magistrates why *he* didn't fall over when Alden looked at *him* but got no answer.

Alden was hauled off to the Boston prison. He spent the long, hot summer there before he managed to escape in mid-September.

Goody Elizabeth Howe belonged to a family that had land disputes with the Putnams. That was never a good sign. She had never met any of the girls accusing her because she lived in Topsfield. She asked her brother-in-law to make the trip to her examination with her because her husband, James, was blind and she didn't want to go alone; he refused, afraid suspicion would then fall on him. She probably had to make the trip by herself.

At Goody Howe's examination, Ann Putnam displayed her hand with a pin stuck in it, and several of the girls started to have fits. The magistrates used the "touch test" to check for Goody Howe's guilt. The idea here was that when a witch touched an accuser who was having a fit, the witch's magic would flow out of the afflicted person and back into the witch, and the fit would end. Of course, an accuser faking their fit could just stop. Goody Howe was forced to touch her supposed victims, and—surprise!—their symptoms immediately eased. She was hauled off to jail even though her husband depended on her to lead him by the hand.

Martha Carrier, who lived in Andover, a town not far from Salem, was Mary Toothaker's sister and Roger Toothaker's sister-in-law. Guilt by association sure seemed to be at play when Goody Carrier and her four children were accused. She was understandably angry and confrontational at her examination, but her snark didn't help her cause.

The afflicted girls claimed to see a menacing man dressed all in black standing near her. When Hathorne asked if she saw the man, Carrier retorted, "I saw no black man but your own presence." Snap!

The afflicted girls roamed around at the examination, stopping to stare into people's faces. Choosing their next victims? Mary Walcott told the magistrates Carrier claimed she'd been a witch for forty years! That was a remarkable claim, considering Carrier was only thirty-eight. (I would have rolled my eyes, but it wasn't an option.) Goody Carrier was bound hand and foot so that she couldn't hurt the girls and was carted off.

She wasn't the only one to be tied up. The Salem jailers bound Goody Carrier's two teenage sons with their heels pulled up against their necks, a ferocious torture technique jailers would employ for hours at a time—and sometimes longer than a day—to elicit confessions. Sure enough, the two boys confessed to witchcraft and even went so far as to testify against their mother! Goody Carrier's **seven-year-old** daughter and **ten-year-old** son also confessed, but without being physically tortured.

EXCUSE ME, SIR—I BELIEVE YOUR DOG IS A WITCH

Goody Carrier and her children's arrests began a flood of accusations and arrests in Andover, including those of several women who confessed to witchcraft when pressured *by their own husbands*! The women may have been too dispirited by lack of support to maintain their innocence, but what explains the men's behavior? Perhaps they were acting because of fear: Maybe, somehow, if their wife was already jailed, attention wouldn't land on them. Nice, right? Before the trials

ended, many Andover men were horrified at their own actions, regretting their "rashnesse and uncharitablenesse." Does it make sense? No. But everyone was trying to figure out some way to be spared. It was a deadly game of chance, and losers got a noose.

Several young people from Andover became afflicted with fits and claimed they were seeing specters. If Salem's girls enjoyed the attention and notoriety witchcraft charges had brought, why wouldn't a youngster from another town, too? Over the course of just a few weeks, Dudley Bradstreet, the justice of the peace in Andover (and son of former Governor Simon Bradstreet), sent perhaps forty accused witches to Andover prison. When he finally refused to issue any more arrest warrants for people accused of witchcraft, he was himself accused of bewitching nine people to death! Bradstreet and his brother, another magistrate, fled Andover before *they* could be arrested.

After Bradstreet had gone, his *dog* was accused of consorting with witches! People claimed to see Bradstreet's specter riding it around town. The poor dog was killed in case it was a witch, too. There was a second canine victim of the witch hunt, also from Andover. Some girls started having fits whenever the dog looked at them, so it was shot.

Sit with that for a minute. They killed two dogs . . . in case they were witches.

When one Boston man was accused of witchcraft by people in Andover, he took immediate legal action and retaliated with a defamation claim against his accusers for a thousand pounds (about $305,000 today). A defamation claim is a lawsuit filed when someone makes a false statement that can damage another person's reputation. It put the accusers on the defensive and at risk of having to pay a large settlement. With money finally involved, the accusers withdrew their claims, which raises the interesting question of whether in Andover, as in Salem, adults may have been behind some of the accusations made by young people. After all, a defamation suit was more dangerous to an adult—who might actually have to pay it.

As far as we know, no one else in Salem or nearby communities accused of being a witch ever thought to file a defamation lawsuit against their accuser. Such legal actions could have saved some lives if they had. Over the course of three months, finally ending in October, more than fifty Andover residents were accused—and there were only about six hundred people in town. If you'd lived in Andover at that time, your chance of being accused of a capital crime was shockingly high. Sobering, isn't it?

Around May 30, Philip English, the Salem Town merchant who fled after his wife, Mary, was arrested, was finally apprehended. At one point he evaded authorities who came looking for him at a Boston friend's home—where he was, in fact, hiding—by crouching behind piles of dirty laundry. English appears to have turned himself in because he thought his escape was hurting his wife's case. His examination was held May 31; a neighbor testified that shortly after an argument he had with English about some property, not only had his son died, but he'd gotten a nosebleed so bad he'd *dripped all over his horse.* What explanation could there be but that English had bewitched him? English was held over for trial and sent to Boston, where his wife was imprisoned. That gave the couple a chance to talk—and to plot.

CHAPTER FIFTEEN

TRIALS BEGIN AT LAST

On May 31 Sarah Good, Rebecca Nurse, John Willard, John and Elizabeth Proctor, Susannah Martin, Bridget Bishop, and Alice Parker were ordered to be moved from the Boston prison and brought back to Salem to stand trial.

The examinations had been humiliating and terrifying—but the very worst that could happen as a result was being jailed. But when a person was found guilty in a formal trial in front of judge and jury, that's when they'd be sentenced. The jury was made up of twelve Salem men who would vote on all the trials for the entire Court of Oyer and Terminer. There was little doubt which way these trials would go or what the sentences would be. People would hang.

Bridget Bishop was the first to be tried.

She was alone, with no defense lawyer. She stood in front of virtually everyone she'd ever known, possibly in the same clothes she'd been chained in for weeks in a damp dungeon.

She probably reeked and had ratty hair. There was social humiliation. Physical pain as muscles immobilized by chains labored to move again. And she would have been terrified.

If you walked in and saw Judge Stoughton, his six associate judges, and the jury, wouldn't you be terrified? I wouldn't, but then again, I can't walk. Do you know me yet? Bridget Bishop will.

The morning of June 2 Goody Bishop was strip-searched by female examiners who claimed at her trial to have found an extra nipple on her body. Whatever it actually was—a mole, a rash, a pimple, a bruise—the jurors took it as evidence of a "witch's mark" used to feed her familiar. They strip-searched her again that afternoon and the mark was gone, and its disappearance, too, was taken to be evidence of witchcraft—not that a small bruise or blemish might have healed.

As they'd done at her examination, Goody Bishop's accusers had fits in the courtroom and accused her of causing them. They mimicked her every gesture and fell down whenever she looked at them.

There was new testimony, too, including that of the Salem man who said Bishop had been responsible for the death of his eldest child through witchcraft fourteen years earlier. (Shortly before his own death, this man admitted he'd lied, but that would be of no use to Goody Bishop.)

Two men who'd done some repairs on Bishop's home claimed they'd found "poppets" in her cellar wall. Poppets were small rag figures, much like voodoo dolls, which could be used to torment a victim. Whether they actually found dolls or just bits of rags didn't matter to the court.

The now-you-see-it-now-you-don't extra nipple, the horrible effect she seemed to have on her accusers whenever she looked at them, the alleged poppets—it was all taken as hard evidence and real proof of witchcraft.

Bridget Bishop was found guilty of witchcraft and sentenced to death.

On June 10, 1692, at eight o'clock in the morning, a ladder was thrown against the gray trunk of a huge oak tree in Salem Village. Bridget Bishop climbed the ladder, and the executioner put a noose over her head and shoved her off. She was the first of twenty people who would be executed.

Not everyone thought the case against Goody Bishop was strong enough to justify killing a woman. One of the associate judges, Nathaniel Saltonstall, resigned after the verdict. As it was explained in the written record of the trial, "he has left the court, and is very much dissatisfied with the proceedings of it."

In Boston, Governor Phips asked several area ministers, including the influential Reverend Cotton Mather (the man who took the afflicted Martha Goodwin into his home and later wrote *Memorable Providences, Relating to Witchcraft and Possessions*) for their thoughts on the situation in Salem. That suggests there were already some concerns about the proceedings. Reverend Mather sent their reply on June 15 in a long document called *Return of Several Ministers Consulted*. They urged Judge Stoughton and his five remaining associate judges to proceed carefully, especially in cases where the accused was of high moral character.

The ministers also urged caution in accepting spectral evidence, "lest by too much credulity for things received only upon the Devil's authority, there be a door opened or a long train of miserable consequences." In other words, they should be cautious about accepting evidence about what specters were doing because specters were witches and you shouldn't trust a witch. At the same time, the ministers urged "the speedy and vigorous prosecution" of the suspects. It wasn't an entirely clear answer.

The next day, June 16, Roger Toothaker died in jail. Now the afflicted girls had Bridget Bishop's blood on their hands—and Toothaker's as well.

THIRTEEN DROWNED OXEN

The court met again on June 29 to judge Sarah Good, Rebecca Nurse, Sarah Wilds, Elizabeth Howe, and Susannah Martin. Evidence from the examinations was admitted at the trials, and the court permitted use of the "touch test"—the one where if fits stopped when an afflicted person was touched, it was taken as proof that the person who touched them was a witch.

At the trial of Sarah Good, new testimony was heard, including from a couple who testified that twice they'd found their broom in an apple tree. The logical conclusion? Goody Good put it there. Another couple testified they'd once taken in Sarah Good and her family but had to ask them to leave six months later "for quietness sake." Soon after, their cattle began to sicken and die. Another man testified he once refused to let Sarah Good in his house when she came begging, fearing she might be carrying smallpox. He said Good "fell to muttering and scolding extremely" and one of his cows "died about the time abovementioned." He and some neighbors couldn't find a cause of death for the cow, so it must have been bewitched to death by Goody Good.

One of the afflicted girls (which one isn't clear) claimed Good's specter had stabbed her with a knife just the day before, and she produced the tip of the blade that had broken off in the attack. Here was clear proof! Yes, it had been a spectral attack, but it was one everyone could accept because of the hard evidence left behind. Unexpectedly, a man in the audience interrupted to say he'd broken his knife the previous day and thrown the tip of it away, and he'd seen the girl now accusing Good standing nearby. He then produced the knife hilt with part of the blade still attached—and it fit with the tip the girl had produced. She was caught in a lie! But after a general reminder from the court to tell the truth, the girl was allowed to continue her testimony. How disgusted must Sarah Good have been at *that*?

Sarah Good was found guilty of witchcraft and sentenced to death.

As Susannah Martin, who openly disbelieved the girls, took the stand, her accusers convulsed until blood ran out of their mouths. The sight must have been shocking! Someone stuck their finger in the ooze and smelled—or possibly licked—it to confirm it was blood. No one thought to question if the girls might have bitten their own tongues to further their cause.

One of Goody Martin's neighbors testified that when he declined to let her borrow his ox, they argued, and shortly thereafter, he'd discovered thirteen of his oxen had jumped into the ocean and drowned. Another neighbor testified Goody Martin's specter appeared to him when he refused to help her husk some corn. He struck the specter with a stick, and soon after that, Martin was said to be unwell! Both accusers thought their stories proved witchcraft. But might these stories have really been spun from the guilty consciences of neighbors who'd refused to help an elderly widow?

Susannah Martin was found guilty of witchcraft and sentenced to death.

"SAY SHE IS A WITCH!"

At her trial, Elizabeth Howe's accusers fell into fits and she was again directed to do the "touch test" to show she was a witch. She had to touch several of the convulsing, screeching girls. Their fits would quiet, but then a few moments later, they would restart, and Goody Howe had to touch them again. It must have been exhausting for everyone. Someone testified that when Goody Howe tried to join the Ipswich church a few years before, some people had opposed her membership and *things began to happen to them*. One family's cow died in a pond. Another's mare looked like it had been beaten. When a neighbor's ox trampled her field, the exasperated Goody Howe said she hoped it would choke, and it did, choking to death on a turnip. Clearly all of this proved Goody Howe was a witch who relished getting her revenge.

Remarkably, twelve people testified in Goody Howe's defense, two of them ministers. One of them testified to accompanying Goody Howe on a visit to a ten-year-old girl whom Howe had allegedly bewitched. The girl hadn't accused Howe, though, and when the minister asked her if the woman had hurt her, the girl said, "No, never," even as her older brother was shouting, "Say Goodwife Howe is a witch, say she is a witch!" from upstairs. Sadly, even weak evidence, strong support, and the ministers' testimony didn't help Goody Howe.

Elizabeth Howe was found guilty of witchcraft and sentenced to death.

Sarah Wilds was the mother of Topsfield Constable Ephraim Wilds, who had arrested Deliverance and William Hobbs a few weeks earlier.

He testified in his mother's defense that he was afraid the Hobbses would accuse his mother as payback because he "almost saw revenge in [Deliverance Hobbs's] face, she looked so maliciously on me" when he'd arrested her. His fears were proved right.

The most gripping testimony against Goody Wilds came from two brothers who recounted a story from *twenty years before*, when they were teenagers. They'd broken their scythe during haying and gone to the Wilds' house to borrow one. Sarah Wilds said they couldn't spare a scythe, but the brothers took one anyway, and Goody Wilds sent her son after them to say his mother demanded they return it immediately or "it should be a dear scythe to us." The brothers kept the pilfered scythe, cut their hay, and proceeded to have one mishap after the other—stubborn oxen, a wheel falling off their wagon, and a load of hay dumped in a stream at the bottom of a hill. Insolence and poor judgment by the teenagers? Or witchcraft by the woman who'd tried to stop them from stealing?

Finally, a young man testified that a year before "about midnight the bed shook and I awakened and saw a woman stand by the bed side which when I well looked seemed to me to be goodwife Wilds which jumped to the other corner of the house and then I saw her no more." Well, that certainly clinched it.

Sarah Wilds was found guilty of witchcraft and sentenced to death.

CHAPTER SIXTEEN

GUILTY UNTIL PROVEN GUILTY

I t was hard to believe Rebecca Nurse could be a witch.

Unlike many of the defendants, Goody Nurse had incredible family support. In the days leading up to her June 30 trial, her husband, Francis, banged on doors across Salem Village, gathering signatures from thirty-nine residents in support of Rebecca. Constable Hathorne's sister was one of them, and so was Samuel Sibley, whose wife had told Tituba to bake that witch cake months ago when only two girls were twitching and no one had yet been accused of witchcraft. Even some of the Putnams signed.

Francis Nurse didn't stop there. He moved aggressively to defend his wife, flipping the tables by introducing testimony against her accusers at her trial. One of Goody Nurse's accusers was Mercy Lewis, the Putnams' maid. A couple who'd employed Lewis a few years before testified the girl wasn't known for telling the truth. Accuser Susannah Shelden's testimony was wildly inconsistent—she kept changing details in her story, just as a person might if they were making it up, rather than simply misremembering. Why was no one questioning the *accusers'* reputations, Francis Nurse asked?

Goody Nurse had an unexpected defender, too—Nathaniel Putnam, Thomas's uncle, who'd been fighting the Nurses for years over a land boundary. He acknowledged Goody Nurse disagreed with her neighbors—namely him—but said she'd raised and educated her family well and that no one had ever suspected her of dealings with the Devil.

Just as they'd done at her examination, the afflicted girls started having fits during Goody Nurse's trial, crying out that Nurse was pinching them and pricking them with pins. Sarah Bibber grabbed her knees and yowled with pain, suddenly displaying pins in her skin. An onlooker who'd been watching Sarah, however, spoke up to say they'd seen Sarah pull the pins from her clothing and shove them in her knees herself. The case could have been thrown out right then—and the accusers with it! But the judges allowed it to continue. Abigail Williams then told of seeing the Devil host a demonic church service with none other than Rebecca Nurse seated beside him.

The strongest evidence against Rebecca Nurse, who was known for her calm demeanor, was supplied by Goody Sarah Holten, who said that three years earlier, a very angry Goody Nurse had confronted Holten's husband, whose pigs were loose, damaging crops in the Nurses' field, and Rebecca threatened to have her son shoot the pigs. The pigs survived, but Holten, who'd been healthy before his pigs wandered into the Nurses' field, soon afterward became ill and died. Now that his widow thought back on it, surely that was the work of a witch.

The jury deliberated.

They returned the verdict: Not guilty.

Could it be? Had Rebecca Nurse just proven her innocence?

IF YOU'D ASKED LOUDER, I'D BE ALIVE

The onlookers were stunned. Her accusers promptly fell into epic fits and one judge told the jury he was disappointed. Another judge asked the jurors to reconsider. Goody Nurse had been in prison with the Hobbses and, apparently, didn't expect them to be at her trial. The judge reminded the jurors that when Deliverance and Abigail Hobbs had been brought into the courtroom, Nurse had been surprised to see them and said, "What, do you bring her? She is one of us." The judge suggested that "She is one of us" meant Nurse was confessing to witchcraft.

It was extraordinarily unusual for judges to send a case back to the jury and ask them to *convict*. Judges did occasionally question jury decisions when a guilty verdict hadn't been proven. But to send a not-guilty verdict back and ask for a conviction? Seems like a dirty trick.

The jurors deliberated again. Unable to come to an agreement, the jury foreman walked up to Goody Nurse and asked what she'd meant by her remark "She is one of us." She didn't reply because she didn't hear him. Later she explained that she'd meant Hobbs was a *prisoner* like her. Unfortunately, the jury took her silence as agreement with the judges' interpretation.

This time, Rebecca Nurse was found guilty of witchcraft and sentenced to death.

In a stroke of remarkable cruelty, on Sunday, July 3, the Salem

Town minister asked his congregation if a convicted witch should be allowed to be a church member. When he put it that way, the answer was clear. The congregation voted unanimously to expel Rebecca Nurse, and that afternoon she was brought to the church shackled and chained, and forced to stand in the center aisle while the minister recited everything she'd supposedly done wrong. Then he excommunicated her—formally kicked her out of the church. As a Puritan, Goody Nurse would have believed this meant she was going to hell. That must have been terrifying to someone who would soon have a noose around her neck.

The Nurse family never gave up hope. Francis demanded copies of all the trial documents as he worked to try to free her. A few days later Governor Phips himself gave Rebecca Nurse a reprieve, meaning that her execution would be postponed indefinitely, which gave Francis more time to try to get the verdict overturned. Governor Phips and Lieutenant Governor Stoughton—who was, don't forget, head judge in the Court of Oyer and Terminer—didn't like or trust each other. Phips granting Nurse a reprieve was likely a little slap at Stoughton.

The afflicted girls went into fits on hearing of the reprieve, and some men in Salem lobbied for Nurse's execution. It was too much. The reprieve was revoked. On Tuesday, July 12, Judge Stoughton signed a warrant for the executions of Sarah Good, Susannah Martin, Elizabeth Howe, Sarah Wilds—and Rebecca Nurse.

On July 19, 1692, the five condemned prisoners were taken to their executions. The afflicted girls headed up a crowd of gawking onlookers mocking and jeering at the women as the grim procession wound its way toward the oak tree in the distance.

The victims that July day were each forced to climb a ladder leaning against the Hanging Tree. The last to die would have seen four swaying bodies in the tree as she made her way up the rungs.

After they were pronounced dead, the women's bodies were cut down and thrown into a rocky crevice. No graves. No headstones. No services said over them. No public grieving to comfort the families. Though they were not supposed to, Rebecca Nurse's grandsons came back that night to retrieve her body so they could bury her in the family plot.

Did anyone even think to tell little Dorothy Good her mother had been hanged?

YOU MUST DIE BECAUSE YOU KNOW WHAT LOCUSTS SOUND LIKE

That didn't end things; it didn't come close. On July 30, Mary Toothaker, now a widow, confessed at her trial, saying she'd been so afraid of attacks by Indigenous people that she'd made a pact with the Devil to save herself.

Mary Toothaker was found guilty of witchcraft and sentenced to death.

Martha Carrier's trial began at ten o'clock in the morning on August 5. Enough people testified that the judges didn't even bring in her two sons who'd been tortured into accusing her. Not using testimony produced through torture made the case against her stronger. A man who'd had a land boundary dispute with Goody Carrier testified that after she threatened him and said he'd be sorry, several of his cattle died and he got painful boils that had to be lanced. According to one particularly damning testimony against her, Satan had promised to make Goody Carrier the "Queen of Hell."

Martha Carrier was found guilty of witchcraft and sentenced to death.

Much of the testimony from Elizabeth Proctor's trial has been lost, but we know several people testified that she'd killed people and the ghosts of the dead (invisible, of course) were accusing her. We also know a woman said Goody Proctor had killed her stepfather because when he got sick, he and his family hadn't asked for Goody Proctor's help. Now Goody Proctor was being blamed for a man's death because she *hadn't* been there and they hadn't asked her to come! How could you win with a trial like that?

The chilling answer, of course, is that you couldn't.

Elizabeth Proctor was found guilty of witchcraft and sentenced to death.

Her husband, John Proctor, was accused at his trial by a man who'd been in pain, and when the pain subsided, took it as proof of witchcraft. Why? Because the afflicted girls had *told* him Proctor's specter had been causing his pain, and it was when Proctor's specter turned his attention away from the man to torment the girls that the man's pain ceased. The man providing the testimony hadn't actually *seen* Proctor's specter do any of that—of course not. But he still testified to it in court.

A defense petition on behalf of John and Elizabeth Proctor was presented to the court. Twenty people had signed it, verifying they'd never suspected the Proctors of bewitching anyone. Another petition was sent in from Proctor's hometown of Ipswich. It had been started by Reverend John Wise, who wrote above the thirty-two signatures a warning that God might permit "Satan to impersonate, dissemble, and thereby abuse innocents." He was saying spectral evidence couldn't be trusted. Wise went on to write, "We speak upon our personal acquaintance and observation" that neither Proctor was guilty of witchcraft. But the petitions didn't sway the court.

John Proctor was found guilty of witchcraft and sentenced to death.

Back in Salem jail to await execution, John Proctor made out a new will in which he didn't include his wife. He was probably expecting her to be killed alongside him, and what was the point of leaving anything to someone who was about to die?

Once he'd made his way to the stand using his canes, elderly George Jacobs Sr.'s trial began with sixteen-year-old John DeRich's testimony that a deceased Salem couple had appeared to him to say Jacobs Sr. had murdered them and the ghostly couple would "tear [DeRich] to pieces if he did not go and declare to Mr. Hathorne that George Jacobs Senior did kill them."

DeRich also reported Jacobs Sr. had once told him not to eat any of his cherries and had tried to get him to sign the Devil's book. These charges were a mixture of the fantastical and the petty, as they were at so many of the witch trials. Jacobs Sr. certainly had *not* tried to get anyone to sign the Devil's book—but he probably *had* told DeRich not to steal his cherries. Was the poor man being accused as payback for being stingy?

George Jacobs Sr. was found guilty of witchcraft and sentenced to death.

What do Martha Carrier, the Proctors, and George Jacobs Sr. have in common besides their death sentences? They'd all voiced skepticism about the afflicted girls' claims, and that marked them as enemies.

Constable John Willard was also a skeptic; he'd refused to make more witchcraft arrests and fled Salem when he was himself accused.

At his trial Willard was not only charged with seventeen-year-old Daniel Wilkins's death, but also with having caused an elderly man's bladder trouble. Two women testified that Willard's wife had told them she'd seen him run up "a steep hill, almost impossible for any man to run up," the implication being Willard must have made a pact with the Devil to achieve such supernatural hill-running powers.

Then Thomas Bailey declared he'd been riding with Willard one night when "I heard such a hideous noise of strange creatures. I was much affrighted for I never had heard the like noise. I fearing they might be some evil spirits I inquired of the said Willard what might it be that made such a hideous noise." At the time Willard said the noise was locusts, but upon reflection Bailey thought it must have been something supernatural.

Constable John Willard was found guilty of witchcraft and sentenced to death.

CHAPTER SEVENTEEN

MORE EXECUTIONS

The August 5 trial of Salem Village's former minister, Reverend George Burroughs, gripped the town. Reverend Increase Mather attended the trial, and if a celebrity like him was in attendance, you knew the trial was a big deal.

The bulk of the allegations against Reverend Burroughs came from people who had themselves confessed to witchcraft. His accusers claimed the minister was the Devil's right-hand man—in an attempt to bewitch all of New England!—and that he'd been in charge of large gatherings of witches. At his examination, accusers had criticized his "supernatural" strength, and now at his trial, someone said strength in that "very puny man" could only be Devil-granted.

About thirty people testified against Reverend Burroughs at his trial. Satan had promised to make him a king, they said. He bragged about being "above the ordinary rank of witches."

He bragged "that he was above a witch for he was a conjuror," Ann Putnam added. And then the trial was interrupted by fits and seizures that left the afflicted girls immobile. They were bitten, they said, proudly displaying their skin, and sure enough, there were teeth marks. The judges examined Reverend Burroughs's mouth and announced his teeth matched the imprints!

One Thomas Ruck reported going out years earlier to gather strawberries with his sister and Reverend Burroughs, who, at one point, wandered off. Ruck and his sister left for home on horseback. Burroughs was on foot, so they thought they'd reach home long before him, but as they neared the house, he suddenly rejoined them with a basket full of strawberries. How could he be so fast? You might assume Burroughs was a fast runner, or simply knew a shortcut. But the testimony alleged wizardry.

Realizing the trial had turned against him, Reverend Burroughs presented the court with a paper written by an English scholar, which claimed "there neither are, nor ever were witches." This was huge! But the court couldn't possibly accept that claim. If it did, it would be admitting it had hanged six innocent people.

Reverend George Burroughs was found guilty of witchcraft and sentenced to death.

Reverend Hale questioned one of the accusers after the trial, indicating doubts about Reverend Burroughs's guilt. He urged her to speak up while Burroughs was still alive if her testimony wasn't true. She claimed it was. And that was that.

One interesting thing about Mary Warren's written testimony against Reverend Burroughs is it contains the very same line Mercy Lewis, Mary Walcott, and Sarah Bibber had used in their depositions in May: "I verily believe in my heart that Mr. George Burroughs is a dreadful wizard and that he has several times tormented me and the aforesaid persons by his acts of witchcraft." And even more interesting? That line is written in *Thomas Putnam's handwriting*. Had Putnam coached the girls to say that? Did the girls even know he included that final line? It wouldn't matter. "Verily believing in their hearts" counted as evidence.

LET'S MURDER HIM, THEN STEAL HIS PANTS

On the evening of August 18, one of his accusers visited Reverend Burroughs in jail and begged his forgiveness for lying at his trial. Reverend Burroughs forgave her and prayed with her.

Five of the condemned—George Jacobs Sr., Reverend George Burroughs, John Proctor, Martha Carrier, and Constable John Willard—were picked up at jail on the morning of August 19 and taken by cart to the Hanging Tree. Like the condemned before them, they each climbed the ladder, had the noose put around their necks, and were pushed.

I was there, at the center of it all. Do you know who I am yet?

How do you climb a ladder if you use two canes? George Jacobs Sr. would have found out. Like the Nurse family had, his family later retrieved his body and properly buried him in the family graveyard. George Jacobs Sr.'s is the only body of the Salem victims that has been found and identified—in part because the skeleton was tall and toothless, as Jacobs Sr. had been.

The crowd thought Martha Carrier—the only woman executed that day—was the most guilty. It was a larger crowd than had gathered in

July. It's unlikely Martha saw sympathy in the faces of her neighbors as the noose was slipped over her head.

Elizabeth Proctor hadn't been brought to the Hanging Tree with her husband John that day because she was pregnant. Was he relieved she wouldn't watch him die—or did he miss the last chance to see her face? We'll never know, but we do know John addressed the crowd from the ladder, praying for pardon of any sins he'd *actually* committed. According to an eyewitness, he was so cool and collected some people doubted his guilt.

Constable John Willard also addressed the crowd and, like Proctor, seemed "very sincere [and] upright."

Because Reverend Burroughs was the most important of the convicted, dignitaries attended his execution, including Reverend Cotton Mather, who'd cautioned against the use of spectral evidence, but was generally enthusiastic about the trials. A couple of out-of-town constables who were moving a suspect dumped their prisoner in a nearby house and took off for the Hanging Tree so they wouldn't miss the spectacle.

We know that as Reverend Burroughs stood on the ladder in the last moments of his life with a noose around his neck, he prayed with such eloquence that some people wept. Then he recited the Lord's Prayer—*perfectly*. Hey, wait a minute—he didn't stumble over the words as witches were said to do. That unsettled the crowd. Could he be *innocent*? The crowd shifted; some people openly questioned his guilt. Would anyone step in to prevent his execution? But *thirty people* had sworn Reverend Burroughs had bewitched them. If public opinion flipped and he were believed to be innocent, those who testified against him could be in danger.

Before anyone could make a move, the afflicted girls shouted that while the minister was reciting the prayer, they'd seen the Devil whispering the words to him. But if the Devil had whispered the Lord's Prayer to Reverend Burroughs, didn't that mean the Devil could, in fact, recite the prayer? And if *the Devil himself* could recite the prayer without faltering, why couldn't a witch do the same thing? It made no sense. But then, Salem made no sense. Finally, someone shoved Reverend Burroughs off the ladder. As his body swung, Reverend Mather spoke to the assembly from horseback, assuring them killing Reverend Burroughs was the right thing to do.

Reverend Burroughs had shown great dignity in his final moments. He wasn't afforded that dignity at his death. A man (in law enforcement, no less!) stripped his body of its shirt and pants—apparently, they were good quality, and he wanted to sell them.

The corpses were dragged by their nooses and tossed in the rocky crevice. Reverend Burroughs was the last person thrown in. It was shallow enough that his chin and hand—and someone else's foot—stuck out.

The crowd left and I stood alone.

THE MINISTER SAYS TO RUN

Because they were wealthy, Philip and Mary English were allowed to rent decent quarters instead of being held in prison—a luxury few prisoners could afford. After their examinations in the spring, they paid extra to live in the house of the Boston jailer. He could still keep an eye on them, but it was far more comfortable than a cell. And they seem to have hired a guard to accompany them so they could walk around town during the day. Ah, the privileges of wealth!

A prominent Boston minister, Reverend Joshua Moody, invited the couple to church on Sunday, August 21, the day before they were to return to Salem for their trial. In his sermon, Reverend Moody read from the book of Matthew 10:23: "If they persecute you in one city, flee to another." The minister's advice was clear—*run*. So they ran. Philip and Mary English disappeared from under the jailer's nose as they fled Boston, headed to New York.

Because fleeing to avoid trial was a crime, the Salem Town authorities were authorized to confiscate the Englishes' property and clean out their lavish home. They took almost everything, including furniture, dishes, Mary's shoes, the bag she used to make pudding, bottles of wine, and more than four hundred thimbles from Philip's shop. They also made off with six pigs and a bob-tailed cow. Altogether, it was a loss to the couple of almost 1,200 pounds ($367,000 today), plus a 400-pound bond against flight, worth more than $122,000 today.

PUT YOUR HAIR IN THE SKILLET

When palm reader and fortune teller Dorcas Hoar came to trial, her minister, Reverend John Hale, testified against her, but that's not surprising—she'd stolen from him. Fourteen years before, Goody Hoar, her husband, William, and their adult children had conspired with Reverend and Mrs. Hale's servant, Margaret, to rob the Hales. Among other things, they'd taken money, pillowcases of flour, and a necklace—one pearl at a time. William and Dorcas Hoar were found guilty of the thefts, after which the Hoars' children beat the Hales' cow to death. Goody Hoar wasn't a sympathetic defendant. Perhaps understanding this, just before her trial came to a close, she confessed to witchcraft.

Dorcas Hoar was found guilty of witchcraft and sentenced to death. Because of her confession, though, Judge Stoughton granted her a reprieve, delaying her trial in order to give her time to see to her soul. The irony here? Goody Hoar actually *was* a criminal—and the one who *didn't* go to the gallows.

Ann Pudeator was tried on September 10. Most of her trial records no longer exist, but we know Mary Warren claimed Pudeator had poisoned her husband after killing his first wife. The reality is that Ann was a widow when a Salem blacksmith, Jacob Pudeator, hired her to take care of his sickly, alcoholic wife. After her death, Pudeator married Ann, but then Pudeator himself died. There was no evidence she killed either Jacob Pudeator or his first wife—but there was also no way to prove that she hadn't. Goody Pudeator begged the judges that "my life may not be taken away by such false evidence and witnesses as these be."

Ann Pudeator was found guilty of witchcraft and sentenced to death.

During her trial, Alice Parker was charged with spectral attacks against Mary Warren and Mary Walcott, including one the previous day. The allegations brought at her May 12 examination were rehashed and then there was testimony given about by a family member of a boy who'd become bewitched. The family put a lock of his hair in a hot skillet to call whomever had bewitched him and Goody Parker arrived at their door. What had she been doing if not bewitching the boy? Selling chickens, Goody Parker replied. The family said she didn't have any chickens with her.

Alice Parker was found guilty of witchcraft and sentenced to death.

Martha Corey was one of the Boston prisoners sent back to Salem for trial, and she was brought before the court on September 9. Not all her trial records survive, but from her examination we know she was a respected church member and shrewd enough to have asked how Ann Putnam knew what her specter was wearing when it allegedly attacked her. Ann couldn't answer. Much of Corey's conviction was based on the behavior of the afflicted girls at her examination, when they claimed her specter was attacking them. *This was completely invisible to anyone else, and yet . . .*

Martha Corey was found guilty of witchcraft and sentenced to death.

Two days later Reverend Parris preached about the "multitudes" of witches in New England, then held a vote to excommunicate Martha Corey. Reverend Parris wanted the trials to go on, but interestingly, the excommunication vote was not unanimous. Some people were taking a stand. That didn't help Corey, though—she was still excommunicated, and probably went to the gallows thinking she was going to hell.

SOMETIMES I'M A BLUE BOAR

A woman named Mary Bradbury was brought to trial on September 6. She'd argued with Ann Putnam Sr.'s father thirteen years before and he'd accused her of witchcraft then. So when the Putnams began hurling witchcraft accusations in the spring of 1692, it wasn't new territory for Goody Bradbury.

One trial witness claimed Goody Bradbury had bewitched a ship he was sailing on. One of Ann Putnam's uncles testified that years earlier Goody Bradbury had turned herself into a blue boar and attacked his horse. Another of Ann's uncles, James Carr, testified that back in the 1670s he'd been courting Rebecca Maverick when one day he showed up at her house to find Goody Bradbury's son, William, there, and Rebecca

no longer interested in him. Carr pointed out that Rebecca went on to marry William. How could Carr have lost her affection if not through witchcraft? Mary Bradbury must have intervened to help her son.

Goody Bradbury had community support—115 people signed a petition attesting to her "courteous and peaceable disposition and carriage, neither did any of us (some of whom have lived in the town with her about fifty years) ever hear or know that she ever had any difference or falling out with any of her neighbors man woman or child."

Mary Bradbury was found guilty of witchcraft and sentenced to death. The high regard of her neighbors must have helped her, however, because at some point Goody Bradbury escaped from jail, something she couldn't have done on her own. She survived the Salem witch trials and died in 1700 in her eighties.

Few documents survive from the trials of Mary Parker, Ann Foster, Wilmott Redd, and Margaret Scott. During that long, hot, drought-stricken summer of 1692, more witches were accused in August than July, and more in September than August. The court was overwhelmed with cases; crops stood unharvested and cows unmilked as their owners languished in overcrowded jails. The lack of surviving documents is due in part to how long ago they were written but may also indicate the speed with which cases were thrown together in late summer. There was no time to dally.

At her examination, widow Mary Parker tried to escape by pointing out that there was *another* Mary Parker from Andover. Hathorne and Corwin conferred briefly: Was this the correct woman? After all, the girls wouldn't have known her by sight. If the other Mary Parker was in attendance, she must have been terrified. The afflicted girls went into convulsions and it was decided that this was indeed the Mary Parker who was bewitching them. Hathorne asked, "How long have you been in the snare of the Devil?"

"I know nothing of it," Goody Parker responded.

It's possible that was the full extent of the questioning—certainly it's all that's recorded. Her trial seems to have been fast and isn't likely to have included more than this flimsiest of evidence.

Mary Parker was found guilty of witchcraft and sentenced to death.

I HOPE YOU NEVER POOP AGAIN

Ann Foster was accused of making Elizabeth Ballard of Andover ill after Ballard's husband, Joseph, asked two of the afflicted girls to visit and see if they thought Elizabeth had been bewitched. They came, agreed that witchcraft was to blame—and named Ann Foster. Elderly and frail, Foster confessed quickly at her July examination. She said Martha Carrier had turned her into a witch and they'd ridden together on a stick to a meeting of witches. Some of Foster's records are missing, but she doesn't seem to have put up a better defense at her trial on September 13, at which the afflicted girls continued to accuse her.

Ann Foster was found guilty of witchcraft and sentenced to death. She died in prison in December.

Wilmott Redd, from the coastal town of Marblehead, was indicted for afflicting Betty Hubbard at various "days and times," and it was recorded that Betty Hubbard "was and is tortured afflicted consumed pined wasted and tormented." It was a broad indictment, short on specifics. It didn't need any. The court also heard testimony that when Goody Redd once had a falling-out with another woman who threatened to take her to court, Redd responded with a vague threat hoping the other woman faced hard times.

A woman from Marblehead testified that five years earlier, a Mrs. Syms had lost some linen and suspected it was stolen by a girl living with the Redds. When confronted, Goody Redd didn't hand over the linen, and Mrs. Syms threatened to go to law enforcement. Goody Redd countered by saying she hoped Mrs. Syms was never able to go to the bathroom again! Sure enough, Mrs. Syms became constipated for a time. What is that if not witchcraft? Or, perhaps, was her testimony simply revenge for linens that went missing half a decade before?

Wilmott Redd was found guilty of witchcraft and sentenced to death.

One allegation against Margaret Scott, from the town of Rowley, included a very serious charge—she'd sickened and eventually killed a man named Robert Shilleto. The couple who testified said Shilleto "often said that [Scott] was a witch and so he continued complaining of Margaret Scott saying that he should never be well so long as Margaret Scott lived."

Another man testified that he owed Goody Scott money and said he'd bring her wood to settle his account, but she didn't think that was fair. Soon after, two of his cattle died, one found standing up on its back legs with its front legs buckled under it, the other in the barnyard with its neck pinned under a board. The man said since that time he'd had some "hard thoughts of this woman and my neighbors told me, something more than ordinary that my cattle died so. And I do verily believe that she is a witch."

Yet another charge against Goody Scott came from six years before, when she'd supposedly asked a neighboring farmer if she could "glean corn in [his] field." The farmer told her to wait and she said he wasn't going to get his corn in that night. Sure enough, the farmer's oxen were difficult that day and he didn't get his corn in.

Margaret Scott was found guilty of witchcraft and sentenced to death.

Samuel Wardwell was a forty-nine-year-old struggling farmer from Andover whose wife was also in jail. At his examination he confessed to witchcraft, saying he liked to tell fortunes, which "sometimes came to pass" and that "he was sensible that he was in the snare of the Devil," but seemed to be puzzling out how he got that way. He admitted that if an animal broke into one of his fields, he used to "bid the Devil take it," and maybe the Devil "took advantage of him by that." Wardwell then began to spin bizarre stories, including that of a "prince of the air" who had some cats and promised to let Wardwell live comfortably. In his rambling confession, Wardwell agreed he'd made a pact with the Devil— but then, in an unusual twist, he said the pact wasn't lifelong but would expire when he turned sixty.

Wardwell didn't mean a word of it! Until that point, confessing had seemed the safest course of action. Those who defended their innocence were tried, convicted, and hanged, while those who confessed were jailed, but not tried—though they were told by the magistrates they were being given extra time to prepare their souls for death. After her crowd-rocking confession during her examination, Abigail Hobbs, the "free spirit" who liked to sleep in the woods, was condemned at her trial but not immediately executed. To Wardwell, confessing probably seemed the smartest way to handle the accusations against him in an effort to save his own life. It didn't help his finances, though; after Wardwell's examination, the constables confiscated his tools and several loads of hay and corn.

At trial Wardwell *recanted his entire confession.* He admitted he'd made the whole thing up! The judges didn't care. He knew they wouldn't, but he'd come to the realization he was going to be killed either way, so he thought he might as well not lie anymore.

Samuel Wardwell was found guilty of witchcraft and sentenced to death.

CHAPTER EIGHTEEN

A PRESSING MATTER

A hanging was scheduled for September 22. Before that could occur, the magistrates had to deal with cantankerous old Giles Corey, who tried something brash that had occurred to no one else—he simply *refused* to be tried.

Back in March, Giles Corey had testified against his own wife and was himself arrested and examined not long after, sent to the Boston prison, and returned to Salem for trial. When he entered the courtroom, the court asked two questions: his plea and whether he agreed to a jury trial. Corey pled not guilty, but he refused to answer the second question. Maybe he refused because the Court of Oyer and Terminer had never found someone not guilty, and he knew that if he was convicted of witchcraft, his estate would be taken by the colony and his children wouldn't inherit anything. Whatever his reason, the frustrated judges ordered Corey taken to a field by the jail on Saturday, September 17.

He was forced to lie on the ground—then they laid boards over his body and piled them with rocks!

The plan? To *squeeze* words out of him. But it didn't work. Corey refused to speak that day. They piled him with rocks again the next day, and Corey *still* refused to agree to a trial, even as his ribs cracked and he was slowly crushed under an agonizing weight. When his tongue extruded from his mouth as he was dying, Sheriff George Corwin shoved it back in with the end of his cane. The only thing the stubborn old man said during his whole ordeal was "More weight."

Giles Corey died around noon on Monday, September 19. Chained up in jail nearby, his wife, Martha, may well have heard his dying gasps.

Giles Corey is the only person in American history who was pressed to death. He hadn't been tried to determine his guilt or innocence—and he'd been tortured to death! This was completely illegal, as no law authorized pressing a defendant. It could have been (yet another) moment for thoughtful, reasonable people to pause and reflect on what was happening, to realize things were going too far. But the spider was still in its web.

Thomas Putnam responded to the whole grisly ordeal by making more accusations and by blaming Corey for his own death. He said his daughter, Ann, had had a vision in which Giles Corey had pressed a servant to death with his feet, and so it was only fitting Corey should die by pressing, too. Years before, Corey had beaten his servant so severely that the man had died, and everyone knew it. Corey had served his punishment for that crime. But even though public skepticism about the trials was growing, few people were courageous enough to take on the Putnams. The trials—and the death sentences—and the hangings—kept going.

RUNG BY RUNG

The last hangings were held on September 22, 1692.

Three days after Giles Corey's horrific death, Martha Corey, Mary Esty, Alice Parker, Mary Parker, Ann Pudeator, Wilmott Redd, Margaret Scott, and Samuel Wardwell were carted to the Hanging Tree.

One by one, the convicted climbed the ladder propped against the oak tree.

The executioner put a noose over the head of the accused witch, cinched it under their chin, then shoved them off the ladder.

The others waited at the bottom until it was their turn to climb.

They all did.

One by one.

I alone felt the weight of the bodies.

HIDE THE KNIVES

On the day Reverend Parris's congregation voted to excommunicate Martha Corey, he'd thundered from the pulpit: "If ever there were witches, men and women in covenant with the Devil, here are multitudes in New England."

At the end of August, Susannah Post confessed to going to a meeting of two hundred witches. Mary Toothaker, who'd confessed at her trial, said she knew of three hundred witches. Could there really be so many witches in New England's small population?

Starting in late summer, some prominent people not afraid of the likes of Thomas Putnam started to voice skepticism about the charges and question how the trials were being run. By early fall, doubts about the proceedings were gaining traction.

And then—perhaps scared, cornered, and knowing the jig would soon be up?—the afflicted girls began saying there were *hundreds* of witches in New England!

Unless something changed, hundreds of people would be carted to the Hanging Tree. It was a sobering thought.

And then the girls overreached.

Taking down Reverend Burroughs had been a coup, as had taking down Goody Rebecca Nurse. It's possible the accusers thought they were unstoppable. After all, they'd been caught lying in court on more than one occasion and they'd not been reprimanded or stopped—the judges still sentenced to death anyone they pointed at.

They accused the two sons of influential former Governor Simon Bradstreet—one of whom, you'll remember, had refused to arrest any more accused witches after sending dozens to jail as Andover's justice of the peace, then fled town, only to have *his dog* accused and killed.

The girls also accused the wife of Reverend John Hale. Years before when she'd discovered their servant, Margaret, had been stealing from them with Goody Dorcas Hoar's assistance, she'd confronted Margaret—who became so belligerent that Mrs. Hale had hidden the kitchen knives. Many of the accusers in Salem were servants; perhaps there were some feelings of solidarity with Margaret at work in accusing Mrs. Hale.

The accusers also pointed at Mrs. Margaret Thatcher—a Boston widow so respected that people called her "Mrs." instead of the usual "Goody." Mrs. Thatcher was the mother-in-law of magistrate Jonathan Corwin (the silent, stern partner of John Hathorne) and was engaged in several ongoing property disputes. Her maid had confessed to witchcraft, and we don't know for certain, but it's possible the girl turned on her employer and accused Mrs. Thatcher.

Astonishingly, the wife of Governor Phips was also named. The most prominent woman in the colony!

Accusations had to be followed up by formal complaints before arrest warrants could be issued, and that didn't happen with Mrs. Thatcher or Lady Phips. Although he'd enthusiastically filed complaints for months, even Thomas Putnam wouldn't swear out a charge against those two women. Nor would anyone else. Had the afflicted girls become overconfident? Sure looks like it.

THE DEVIL CONFUSED ME

Rumors circulated for a time about the wife of Reverend Increase Mather being a witch. The wife of the distinguished minister who'd brought back a new charter from the king's own hand? Preposterous! The rumors were ignored. Reverend Mather had begun to question the trials, but hadn't said so publicly. Instead, he published a book called *Cases of Conscience Concerning Evil Spirits Personating Men*. In it he wrote that the "touch tests" were "the Devil's testimony" and that the Devil could take the form of innocent people. So what was he saying? Spectral evidence was unreliable! This work by such a highly regarded man discredited the trials and undoubtedly helped slow them down. He didn't say that any of the people who'd been executed were not guilty—but he did maintain the dog who'd been shot had been innocent.

After Increase and Cotton Mather, Samuel Willard was the most prominent minister in Boston. He wrote about the events in Salem in his widely respected tract, *Some Miscellany Observations on Our Present Debates Respecting Witchcrafts*, raising the question of whether the Devil might appear in the shape of an innocent person. This was a question many defendants had raised at their own trials—only to be ignored by people in authority and distracted by shrieking girls having fits. Now here was an influential figure asking the very same question, and it was pivotal. Multiple people had already been hanged because of these apparitions. But what if the specters were *not* Goody Nurse or old George Jacobs Sr. or Goody Corey? What if it was the *Devil* taking their shape? What if the Devil made it *look* like your neighbor was pinching you, *but it wasn't really her?*

Reverend Willard also wrote that during their confessions to witchcraft, people who named other witches—a mainstay of the Salem witch examinations and trials—were utterly unreliable. After all, if someone was a witch working for the Devil, wouldn't they lie about something like that? The issue with specters taking your shape and with confessed witches naming names is that the person whose word you're relying on is a witch! How could anyone trust such testimony?

In their writings, Reverend Increase Mather and Reverend Willard did say judges and juries weren't to blame, with Reverend Mather making the point that if any innocent person had been convicted—and he was quick to say he was sure none had been!—the fault was surely with the Devil for confusing everybody.

"I WOULD SOONER BITE MY FINGERS' ENDS"

The General Court in Boston was to meet in a specially arranged session on October 12 to discuss the trials in Salem. Four days before that session, Boston-born scientist and merchant Thomas Brattle wrote a compelling letter against the trials to an unnamed minister (probably Reverend Increase Mather). It was copied and widely circulated throughout Boston. Brattle opened his letter with great respect to the authorities involved: "I would sooner bite my fingers' ends than willingly cast dirt on authority, or any way offer reproach to it." He then went on to agree with Reverend Mather and Reverend Willard that the "touch test" was unreliable. "I suppose his Honor never made the experiment, whether there was not as much virtue in his own hand, as there was in [a defendant's], to cure by a touch." In other words, wouldn't the "touch test" work if *anybody* touched an afflicted girl—so long as she couldn't see who it was? The touch tests worked because the fits were entirely voluntary, and the afflicted girls could end them whenever they wanted. They didn't prove the person whose touch stopped convulsions was a witch—they proved the girls were lying.

He also demanded an explanation for how alleged witches could cause the girls' fits by looking at them but didn't cause fits in other people when they looked at *them*. (This was the very question the accused John Alden posed to the magistrates at his examination, to which he got no response.) Brattle went on to criticize the Court of Oyer and Terminer's reliance on confessions of accused witches, uncorroborated visions of accusers, and the finding of a witch's mark. A witch's mark could look like anything and be anywhere on a person; Brattle pointed out that few people had no mark of any sort anywhere on their body.

Brattle slammed the practice of having the afflicted girls consult on cases in or from other communities, recounting the story of a Boston man who'd brought his sick child to Salem "on purpose that he might consult the afflicted about his child; which accordingly he did." The afflicted girls named two women who were hurting his child and the man went to the Boston justices for an arrest warrant, but was denied. Brattle said Reverend Increase Mather "took occasion severely to reprove the said man; asking him whether there was not a God in Boston, that he should go to the Devil in Salem for advice." *Oh, burn!* That's some fine seventeenth-century trash talk. "This consulting of these afflicted children about their [illness]," Brattle observed, "was the unhappy beginning of the unhappy troubles at poor Andover."

Brattle then went on to ask, if witchcraft was such a bad crime that you executed people for it, why weren't magistrates arresting accused persons who were related to *them*? Why weren't they trying to recapture wealthy people who'd bribed jailers to let them escape? He pointed out that in other crimes serious enough to be punished by death, if someone escaped, the authorities tried harder to find them. Why not witchcraft?

Brattle made excellent points.

Perhaps the strongest point he made pertained to the problem with the accusations themselves: When one of the afflicted girls accused someone they'd never met, they only knew who their tormentor was *because that person's specter told them.* Just as Reverend Mather said in his tract, Brattle said any court that prosecuted a person who was identified by a witch's specter was letting the Devil testify. "I think it will appear evident to any one, that the Devil's information is the fundamental testimony," Brattle wrote. Could you trust what a witch said? Brattle's answer was unequivocally no.

The skeptics and doubters had spoken! But would they *do* anything?

"A SUPPOSED WITCHCRAFT"

As a result of that special court session on Wednesday, October 12, Governor Phips decided to temporarily stop all court activity in Salem. No more arrests; no more examinations; no more trials. He even ordered people to stop publicly discussing what was happening in Salem because it could cause "needless disputes."

By that date, however, Reverend Increase Mather's *Cases of Conscience Concerning Evil Spirits Personating Men* and his son Reverend Cotton Mather's *Wonders of the Invisible World* were both circulating as manuscripts. Where the father was slamming the Salem prosecutions, the son urged *more* prosecutions, suggesting the witch conspiracy might extend even further than was yet imagined.

Governor Phips suspended the trials in part for self-preservation. The new skepticism of the trials could endanger his position, and his political enemies could use the unstable situation in Salem against him. On top of that, Rebecca Nurse's husband had not stopped pressuring the governor to end the trials before more innocents were killed.

Doubts about the witchcraft allegations were rising, but belief in the existence of witches was still strong and widespread. The trials were just on hold—they would resume. And although there would be different rules going forward, so a defendant might now have a chance at acquittal, the accused could still be found guilty. The penalty was still death. And the Hanging Tree still stood at the edge of town.

Also on October 12, Governor Phips wrote his first letter to the English government informing them of the witchcraft crisis—and distancing himself from it, even to the point of lying to his superiors. He claimed he'd been out of the area fighting the crown's enemies during most of the crisis, when in fact he'd been in Boston most of the time. He asked for guidance from London, but that wouldn't arrive for a long time.

On October 18, twenty-six men from Andover petitioned the governor on behalf of their wives, who had confessed under pressure—

often from their husbands themselves. The women—and their husbands—now regretted their actions. Governor Phips may have begun to understand how much weight the court had given spectral evidence. Perhaps the retractions of confessions influenced the governor as he considered the future of the Court of Oyer and Terminer. When trials did resume, he forbade the use of spectral evidence.

Starting on October 12, people newly accused of witchcraft were ordered released on bail rather than being sent to jail. Some people who had already been imprisoned were released, too, once their families paid their jail fees. Those people who had no family, or who were destitute, had to stay in prison until their fees were paid. How frustrating would it be to have been accused of something shocking you didn't do, have a court accept spectral evidence against you, be jailed in filthy conditions and held in heavy chains, and when you were finally released—you couldn't go because you were required to pay for it, and you weren't able to!

The accusers continued to contort, shout, and point fingers, but they didn't have the same power they had had in the spring.

In October the town of Gloucester, almost as far from Salem as Boston, asked for help from Salem's afflicted girls. It must have been an exciting trip for the girls and a compliment to their expertise. The girls were brought to Gloucester to aid in a witchcraft investigation by confirming spectral activity. This resulted in four people being imprisoned.

The girls returned to Gloucester in November at the request of a man who was afraid his dying sister's illness had been caused by a witch. On their journey to Gloucester, the girls stopped at a bridge in Ipswich across which an elderly woman was walking. The girls pointed at her and then fell into fits, throwing themselves about, lolling their tongues out, and shouting they were being pinched and pricked. Everyone simply ignored them. The girls had no choice at that point but to stop their antics, get up, brush themselves off, and continue on their way. When they reached the man who'd asked for their help, the girls agreed with his assessment of his sister's condition and named three people whose specters were tormenting her. But this time, the three they named were not imprisoned and stayed free on bail. This was surely another indication the girls' influence was waning.

ENDING THE COURT OF OYER AND TERMINER

In a direct rebuke to the Court of Oyer and Terminer, on October 26 the General Court announced a day of fasting and a meeting of ministers to decide how to deal with witchcraft allegations. Three days later Governor Phips ended the Court of Oyer and Terminer altogether. A few weeks later, on November 25, the General Court created a Superior Court, but this new court wouldn't have a session in Salem for a year. Would the accused have to wait that long to learn their fate?

The Superior Court managed to set up an extra session at the beginning of the year to try people accused of being witches. Governor Phips once again appointed his lieutenant governor, William Stoughton, to be its chief judge, with three associate judges who'd also served on the Court of Oyer and Terminer. The structure might have been different, but the personnel hadn't changed much.

The Superior Court special session began on January 3 to hear witchcraft cases—and charges were immediately dropped against thirty defendants. Good news!

Twenty-six defendants were tried for witchcraft. Twenty-three were found not guilty. Even better news! This meant it was possible to be tried for witchcraft and *not be convicted.* That was because spectral evidence could no longer be used and because the new charter allowed men who weren't church members—and who were less likely to convict—to serve on juries now.

Rebecca Jacobs, George Jacobs Sr.'s daughter-in-law, was the first person tried by the Superior Court session. She pled not guilty—the age of confessions was over. And while the afflicted girls were undoubtedly present, no one bothered to record what they did. Goody Jacobs was found not guilty and could leave jail whenever her jail fees were paid—which wasn't until March.

Goody Sarah Cloyce was also spared. She was tried separately from her sisters, Rebecca Nurse, who perished in the first group to hang, and Mary Esty, who hanged on September 22, and all charges against her were dismissed in January 1693. What a long ordeal for that family! After five months in chains, she was freed but had trouble moving around. She lived for another ten years. Did she think of her hanged sisters whenever the wind made the boughs of the Hanging Tree creak? I know I did.

JUDGE STOUGHTON WANTS YOU TO HANG

While most people were trying to stop the cart from making another trip to the Hanging Tree, Judge Stoughton was trying to grease its wheels. He continued to trust spectral evidence—even though influential ministers and scientists had said it was useless and Governor Phips had *forbidden its use!* Stoughton announced February 1 would be a hanging day, ordered graves to be dug, and signed an execution warrant for Sarah Wardwell, whose husband, Samuel, had been hanged in September even after recanting his confession. Goody Wardwell did not recant her confession, but that didn't prevent Stoughton's court from convicting her and ordering her death.

Stoughton also signed execution warrants for accused witches Elizabeth Johnson Jr. and Mary Post. And in a fit of temper, he ordered one acquitted woman, Sarah Bridges, to put up a bond of a hundred pounds (more than $30,000 today) to ensure that she appeared in court again the next day to prove her good behavior. Again, this woman had been found *not guilty*—but Stoughton didn't like the verdict.

Some good news came again in the form of an intervention from Governor Phips, who overrode Stoughton's orders and reprieved Wardwell, Johnson, and Post, who'd been found guilty. He also reprieved five other defendants who'd been convicted the previous year by the disbanded Court of Oyer and Terminer. These were not full pardons—which would have meant the eight wouldn't be executed—but it did calm things down for the time being. Stoughton was so enraged when he heard the news that he shouted and stormed off the bench. You read that right—he had a small tantrum because he didn't get to hang people.

After the January trials displayed how much harder it had become to prove witchcraft charges in court, accusations of witchcraft fell sharply. By the end of February 1693, Governor Phips considered the witchcraft epidemic to be over.

Of the hundred and fifty or so accused people who'd been "released" on paper, but who remained in jails for unpaid fees, some would die there. Elderly Goody Lydia Dustin couldn't pay her jail fees and died on March 10, just four weeks after she'd been found innocent and was free to go.

A stranger paid the fees for George Jacobs Sr.'s granddaughter, Margaret, because he felt sorry for her—but later sued her to get the money back. People in Salem hadn't stopped being contentious and snappish.

Tituba had been in jail longer than anyone. Reverend Parris never paid her jail fees and she languished behind bars until someone finally paid them, in effect buying her, as she was still an enslaved woman. We know she left Massachusetts and that in May her case was dismissed, but the rest of her journey is lost to history.

In April 1693 the Superior Court met in Suffolk County, which contained Boston, and all the defendants brought to court were exonerated, including John Alden, who'd escaped from jail in September. He was acquitted by proclamation even though he wasn't there. Alden lived another nine years. Governor Phips referred to what had happened the previous year as "a supposed witchcraft," and in May, he ordered all witchcraft defendants still in jail to be released. (As soon as they paid those jail fees.)

The witch trials were well and truly over.

CHAPTER NINETEEN

A TRAGIC LEGACY

The Salem witch hunt was a large, sprawling, frenzied affair involving hundreds of people that lasted more than a year. Many people died. Many barely survived. Many went on as if nothing had happened.

There's a natural interest in the people who lost their lives, but there's a whole cast of characters who survived and who aren't talked about very much. Those accused people who weren't executed suffered greatly and so did their families. The witch hunt cost lives, and it cost time with loved ones, homes and property, livelihoods, money, productivity, and reputations. The toll on everyone's mental health must have been staggering.

That's most obvious in what happened to precious little Dorothy Good. She was only four years old when she was separated from her mother, was accused of being a witch, saw her little sister die, and was chained in a dungeon for months

in chains so heavy she would have had trouble moving. It was more than any child should ever have to go through and, tragically, Dorothy lost her mind and was unable to care for herself for the rest of her life. Dorothy Good didn't hang, but her life was still taken from her.

Hundreds of people had been without a family member for weeks or months. If one parent was jailed, the other had to do all the childcare and all the work on the farm. And there were cases like those of tavern owners Edward and Sarah Bishop, whose household goods and animals were confiscated when they were charged and whose twelve children were left completely on their own with nothing. Neighbors took them in, but that would have been difficult for them—and traumatic for the kids.

The financial costs were enormous. Taxes skyrocketed to pay for the costs related to the trials, and expenses added up. For example, on February 16, 1693, Governor Phips and his council authorized forty pounds ($12,225 today) as partial payment to Mary Gedney, a Salem tavern keeper who'd provided drinks to jurors and witnesses testifying at the trials.

But that was nothing compared to the expenses of people who'd been accused. Their property and goods were seized as soon as they were *charged*, not when they were convicted or executed. That meant well over a hundred people *who were never convicted* still lost their property and were reduced to poverty.

Elizabeth Proctor gave birth on the Boston prison floor on January 27, 1693, to a boy, John Proctor III, and she was freed in May 1693. Devastatingly, John Proctor had made out that new will leaving nothing to Elizabeth, and she lived in poverty for several years after her release. Eventually, her legal rights to own property were restored and her dowry—the property she'd brought to the marriage—was returned to her, but she never inherited anything from her husband.

George Jacobs Jr. had the horrible experience of seeing his father hanged, and his wife and daughter, Margaret, imprisoned for months. Once they were released, George and his family were able to stay in Salem, but any inheritance from his father had been confiscated when he'd been accused. George's own costs were staggering, which was why someone else paid Margaret's jail fee. The family was reduced to poverty.

I'M MAD ABOUT MY BOB-TAILED COW

Mary English became an invalid and died in 1694. She was only forty-two years old. Her husband, Philip, survived the witch hunt only because he'd fled. He was furious his estate had been confiscated and it especially enraged him to see his bob-tailed cow in Sheriff George Corwin's yard. When Sheriff Corwin died in 1696, English threatened to steal his body and return it to the family only when he got back at least some of the value of the property Corwin had seized from him. English repeatedly refused to pay his church taxes, criticized the clergy, and in 1722 was indicted for calling Nicholas Noyes a murderer, blaming him for the deaths of Rebecca Nurse and John Proctor. Noyes was one of the men in the Putnam camp who frequently accused his neighbors. He'd also been dead for twenty-one years! Clearly English knew how to hold a grudge.

When English was on his deathbed in 1736, his family persuaded him to forgive Noyes. He did so, to clear his conscience before he died, but announced, "But if I get well, I'll be damned if I forgive him!"

Old enmities could die hard—and that was a problem if you lived in

Salem Village in 1693 or the following few years. If you'd been an accuser and now thought the people you'd helped hang had been innocent, how could you look their families in the eye as you passed them at the market? And if you'd seen a family member taunted by the afflicted girls and then make that last, long fall off the Hanging Tree, how could you pass the accusers without clobbering them on the head? How could you sit next to them at church?

A few witnesses eventually admitted they'd lied; many didn't. Reverend Samuel Parris continued to believe in the guilt of the accused. For the families of the executed, attending his church services must have been excruciating. Many hurt feelings settled on Reverend Parris, which, of course, he felt was incredibly unfair. This was a man who'd had his feelings hurt about firewood, after all.

I'M NOT SAYING YOU'RE A LIAR, BUT YOU ARE

In March 1693 men from Rebecca Nurse's family led a group to confront Reverend Parris and try to settle their differences, which they felt the Bible called them to do. But they were so angry with him that it was incredibly difficult—and the minister claimed their complaints were slander. The next month Reverend Parris met with the "disaffected men," as he called them, at Ingersoll's Tavern an hour after sunrise. They read out their long list of complaints, and though they didn't quite call Parris a liar, they didn't quite not call him one, either. The Salem Village church squabbled over the fate of its minister, and the "disaffected men" finally ousted Reverend Parris in 1697. His ailing wife had died the previous year. It's unclear if he ever got his back pay. Betty married in 1710, had four children, and died in 1760.

Slowly, slowly, social relations healed and mended. People found their own way forward. In many homes one family member had accused another—husbands against wives; children against mothers—and now, somehow, they sat across the table from each other at dinner.

In June 1693, less than a year after Reverend George Burroughs was hanged, the jury foreman became the guardian of Reverend Burroughs's sons. The same month, Salem Village saw a wedding between John Wilds, the widower of hanged Sarah Wilds, and Mary Jacobs, the widow of hanged George Jacobs Sr. When Reverend Burroughs's own widow remarried, Reverend Cotton Mather performed the ceremony.

Inexplicably, the witchcraft trials and aftermath did nothing to hurt the political careers of most of the authorities involved. Lieutenant Governor William Stoughton won reelection handily. In fact, everyone who'd served on the court that oversaw the witchcraft trials was reelected in May 1693. Magistrates John Hathorne and Jonathan Corwin continued in their roles for twenty more years, into their seventies.

Governor William Phips did not fare as well. He sailed to England in February 1695 and was promptly arrested—the charges are unclear, but it was probably a financial matter. He caught the flu in jail, and although he was released on bail, he died on February 18.

For the most part, people in Salem simply didn't talk about what had happened in 1692 and 1693. In addition to deliberately not remembering, some of the witch-trial advocates altered the historical record. Reverend Samuel Parris kept church records that included deaths among his parishioners, but he never listed anyone executed during the witchcraft trials. Thomas Putnam, who did more than anyone to keep the witch hunt going, personally rewrote Salem Village's records, completely omitting the period between January 27 and December 7, 1692. He never apologized.

When they wanted to kill their neighbors, they came to me. Do you think I'm a judge? A law book? The Devil himself?

I am the Hanging Tree. Today you won't see any evidence I ever existed—there's nothing left aboveground. But my roots are still there, waiting for someone to water me.

Evil does exist in the world. But it goes about on two feet, not on a broomstick.

RESTITUTION

After the trials ended and as people were released from prison, they began to petition the Massachusetts Bay Colony legislature for repayment of their seized property and the restoration of their good names and reputations. Reverend Cotton Mather himself urged repayment.

The June 13, 1700, petition of a woman named Abigail Faulkner (whose examination and trial records are lost) declares she continued to live, but "only as a malefactor convict upon record of the most heinous crimes that mankind can be supposed to be guilty of, which besides its utter ruining and defacing my reputation," left her vulnerable to future witchcraft charges.

The Massachusetts legislature considered Faulkner's petition and overturned her conviction as well as those of some other people it didn't name, saying their reputations were restored. The legislature also looked at the trial evidence from 1692 and was appalled. The Salem witch trials was the last time spectral evidence was ever allowed in a trial. It was outlawed going forward.

Finally, in late 1710, the Massachusetts General Court agreed to reverse the convictions of people who had been hanged—but only if their families had petitioned for the reversal. If a family hadn't petitioned, their relative's conviction wasn't reversed. Some people wouldn't have wanted to keep thinking about it eighteen years later or were so busy trying to scratch out a living after all the property seizures that they didn't have the energy to deal with writing petitions.

In October 1711, the colony granted financial restitution to the victims in the amount of 578 pounds, 12 shillings ($177,000 today). It wasn't nearly enough—accused people had been charged for everything, including the paper on which their pardons had been written!—and the money was awarded somewhat haphazardly. The heirs of John Proctor, who'd been fairly wealthy, got 150 pounds ($46,000 today), which was by far the largest award. The families of George Jacobs Sr. and Reverend George Burroughs each got a sizable settlement, though Reverend Burroughs's widow took off with the money and left her stepsons destitute. As late as 1750 his grandsons were still petitioning for further repayment. There didn't seem to be much logic involved with the size of the smaller awards. Abigail Hobbs, who'd been accused— and confessed—but was also an accuser, was still awarded ten pounds ($3,056 today).

Thankfully, the names of most victims were cleared.

The reputations of those who accused their neighbors or prosecuted the trials were irreversibly damaged. Betty Parris, Sarah Churchill, Mary Walcott, and Mercy Lewis all left Salem Village eventually. What of Abigail Williams, who was the first to be afflicted? We don't know what happened to her. She disappears entirely from the historical record. It's been suggested she didn't live long enough to marry—just like the egg white in the Venus glass predicted.

Thomas Putnam and his wife died within two weeks of each other in 1699 and left their daughter, Ann, to care for her nine siblings. She never married. In August 1706 Reverend Joseph Green, who had replaced Reverend Parris, read from the pulpit a statement Ann wrote confessing her sins—including her involvement in the witchcraft trials—while she stood silently. Ann had testified against seventeen of the nineteen people who'd hanged. She hadn't done so out of ill will, she said in her statement, but because of a "delusion of Satan," admitting "I have been instrumental . . . [in] the guilt of innocent blood."

Reverend Green also tried to reconcile his congregation—by rearranging seating in the meetinghouse and putting the Putnam and Nurse families next to each other!

In January 1697 Massachusetts observed a day of fasting to atone for the wrongs of the past. Judge Samuel Sewall, who'd been one of the associate judges at the trials, apologized publicly in Boston for his role in the witchcraft trials, saying he was ashamed of himself. He was the only judge to do so. Twelve trial jurors also signed an apology.

In 1957, the state of Massachusetts officially apologized to the descendants of those accused in the Salem witch trials for the episode—more than two hundred fifty years after it happened.

No one put up a monument to the victims for three hundred years. A memorial in central Salem was finally erected in 1992. Writer and World War II Holocaust survivor Elie Wiesel dedicated it, saying, "If I cannot fight the hatred all over the world at least I can fight hatred somewhere, in one person, in me." On July 19, 2017, the 325th anniversary of the hanging of Rebecca Nurse and the others who died that day, a memorial was dedicated at the general site of the executions, now called Proctor's Ledge. It includes the names of the nineteen people who were hanged there, where I stood. Murdered on me.

Bridget Bishop, the first person to hang, had not been included in the 1710 pardon; the Massachusetts state legislature cleared her name in 2001, along with those of Susannah Martin, Alice Parker, Wilmott Redd, and Margaret Scott.

Finally, in 2022, Elizabeth Johnson Jr. was the last of the Salem victims to be exonerated. Johnson had confessed when interrogated but was not hanged and lived into her seventies. The Massachusetts legislature officially exonerated her after Carrie LaPierre, an eighth-grade civics teacher at North Andover Middle School, and her students took up the cause to clear her name.

CHAPTER TWENTY

SALEM'S ECHOES

The tragic events at Salem have left a deep mark on American culture.

In the years immediately following the witch hunt, people in Salem Town (now called Salem) and Salem Village (now the town of Danvers) avoided talking about it to anyone. (I understood that. I was ashamed, too.) But today, the witch hunt and trials are an economic mainstay of these Massachusetts communities, as Salem and Danvers do a brisk business in witch tourism. The Salem High School sports teams are the Witches, and their logo shows a witch on a broomstick.

It is because of Tituba's testimony that Americans think witches fly. In 1692 people in England didn't believe witches flew through the sky, on broomsticks or otherwise, but Tituba's words gave American witches their power of flight: "We ride upon sticks and are there presently." Tituba also

established the black cat as an animal associated with witches. When she included a "black cat" among the list of witches' familiars during her testimony, it didn't stand out to the audience because at that time black cats weren't associated with witches any more than other animals of any color. But today, you'll find broomsticks and black cats on Halloween decorations and costumes.

The events at Salem were so shocking, tragic, and inexplicable they've caught our imagination for three and a half centuries. Songs, plays, and poems have been written about the witch trials.

One of Salem magistrate John Hathorne's descendants was so ashamed of Hathorne's role in the trials that he added a "w" to his last name so it wouldn't look like they were related. That descendant was the famous writer Nathaniel Hawthorne (1804–1864), who wrote *The Scarlet Letter* (1850), which includes themes of sin, redemption, and the consequences of intolerance, and *The House of the Seven Gables* (1851), which deals in part with the legacy of guilt from the witch trials.

A PIMPLE POPS

Perhaps the best-known written work on Salem is Arthur Miller's play *The Crucible*, which premiered in January 1953, focusing on a fictionalized John and Elizabeth Proctor. Though set in seventeenth-century Massachusetts, the play intended to draw the audience's eye to what was happening in the United States in the 1950s. The country was in the grips of a vicious smear campaign called McCarthyism, named for Senator Joseph McCarthy, a Republican from Wisconsin, and which is often referred to as a "witch hunt."

In February 1950, Senator McCarthy announced that the State Department, a federal agency that leads the United States' foreign policy, was "thoroughly infested with communists," and he had a list of names of communists in the government. It wasn't true, but the more frequently and loudly the senator shouted it, the more people started to believe it. He was employing a technique called "the big lie"—something so outrageous you can't believe anyone would actually lie about it.

McCarthy's accusations created a climate of fear and distrust, and this "Red Scare" (communists often used the color red) laid the groundwork for him to make baseless allegations, intimidate people, and imply *guilt by association*. That means you're suspected of something because you know someone who's guilty or suspected of the same thing—just as people in Salem were more likely to be accused of witchcraft if someone in their family had been. As part of the Red Scare, an organization called the House Un-American Activities Committee (HUAC) was formed to haul professors, writers, actors, and directors to testify about any communist connections and to name names. Many people lost their jobs. Some died by suicide. So many lives were ruined.

McCarthy's influence grew as he repeated his lie, and he became so powerful that public officials around the country were afraid to speak out against him. Sounds like Thomas Putnam, doesn't it? President Dwight Eisenhower called McCarthy a "pimple on the path of progress," but even he did so privately. Finally in 1954 McCarthy overstepped, just as Salem's afflicted girls had when they accused Mrs. Thatcher and Governor Phips's wife of witchcraft. In this case, Senator McCarthy took on the US Army! He said it was riddled with communists, but he and HUAC were unable to come up with any solid evidence. Congress passed a motion of condemnation of McCarthy in December 1954. That didn't do much to him except hurt his reputation, but it was enough to stop McCarthyism.

The Salem witch scare is a touchstone in American culture—everyone's heard of it. For some people, it's more than a part of the nation's past; it's part of their family's heritage, too. Walt Disney was a descendant of Reverend George Burroughs. The famous Civil War nurse Clara Barton descended from Sarah Cloyce. President Chester Arthur was descended from Susannah Martin and John Proctor. Mary Bradbury's kin include poet Ralph Waldo Emerson, science fiction writer Ray Bradbury, and astronaut Alan Shepard. Author Louisa May Alcott was descended from Judge Samuel Sewell. The descendants of people involved in the Salem witch trials number in the millions. Maybe they even include you.

The events in Salem can seem very distant to us today, but the conditions that led to the tragedy there can occur anywhere and in any century—even now. A community was divided between two groups. Families in one town were bitterly envious of successful families in another town. Girls had no outlet for fun and weren't listened to by adults. And some members of the community were seen as less important—like the enslaved woman, Tituba, and the strange muttering woman, Sarah Good.

Part of the reason the witch hunt in my town, Salem, went on so long, and gathered steam as it went, was that there was no way to back down. If the accusing "afflicted girls" were caught faking their fits, they'd have been in a world of trouble. But the thing is, they already were. Theirs was a world of boredom, limited opportunities, bitter adults, and sudden explosions of violence set against a backdrop of religious fervor, judgment, and a very real fear of going to hell. People were willing to think the worst of their neighbors, to accuse them of terrible crimes, and, in the process, to spill innocent blood themselves.

WITCHCRAFT IN CONTEXT

Salem was not the first place to experience mass hysteria and psychoses about witches. Witch hunts and trials as we think of them today are a product of the Early Modern period (roughly 1450–1700), when thousands of Europeans were tried for witchcraft. People had been accusing their neighbors of witchcraft since ancient times, but the number of witchcraft accusations rose sharply in the late sixteenth and early seventeenth centuries, then declined into the early 1700s, when they mostly stopped.

Historian Geoffrey Parker points out that the rise in accusations corresponds to the Little Ice Age, a period of climate change from 1550 to 1700. Among other charges, witches were blamed for unnatural weather. People believed natural disasters were caused by divine anger at human failings—someone had done something to turn God's vengeful eye on the community—and scapegoats had to be found. Accusations peaked in the coldest decades. As temperatures dipped, areas where land was poor and agriculture was always vulnerable felt the impact earliest and hardest, and those areas had some of the highest rates of witchcraft allegations. In the 1640s, the Scottish Parliament blamed witchcraft for heavy precipitation that led to a poor cereal harvest. Two decades earlier, in the spring of 1626, a hailstorm in Germany led to the torture and execution of *nine hundred people* suspected of causing the disaster through paranormal means. And you thought Thomas Putnam was bad.

Many of the people accused of harming others in their community were women, especially older women, and they were usually outsiders in some way. Older women who'd finished raising their families and may have been widowed needed more financial help and were likely doing less work at that point in their lives, so they could be seen as a drag on resources during a time of scarcity. Additionally, in the years and months before the witch outbreak in Salem, New England towns had been flooded with refugees from the wars with Indigenous nations, further straining resources. Did you notice how many of the Salem witchcraft allegations were based on someone asking for help, being denied, and then being accused of witchcraft when something bad happened to the denier? Guilty consciences—and fears of paranormal payback—underlaid many of the accusations.

In addition to the Little Ice Age, the period from 1517 to about 1547 was shaken by religious change and torn by religious wars, which spawned a surge in witchcraft allegations. In this span of only thirty years, large swaths of Europeans protested what they saw as corruption in the Roman Catholic Church, tried to reform it, and then split off into a new reform religion, eventually called "Protestant." It was a time of chaos and violence, which breeds suspicion and doubt.

After the Protestant Reformation, interest in religious conformity increased—and so did the fear of witchcraft. Something "other" was out there, and it was dangerous. Trials and executions shot up in the 1590s in many parts of Europe. There were large-scale witch hunts, too, including in Scotland from 1590 to 1597 and in the German Catholic states in the 1610s and 1620s. In Europe, a trial did not automatically lead to conviction as it did in Salem—only about half of all defendants were found guilty. Conviction did lead to execution, however, perhaps following the biblical injunction in the book of Exodus 22:18, "Suffer not a witch to live." While the Salem victims were hanged, most convicted witches in Europe were burned at the stake.

By around 1630, skepticism in educated circles reduced the number of witch hunts, and trials declined in the second half of the seventeenth century. Sweden had one big witch hunt in the 1670s, and Poland burned witches on a large scale into the 1700s. Even so, Salem's witch hunt was relatively late and came in a period that was—finally—leaving witches behind.

Perhaps most importantly, the people in Salem were living in an age without science. The period of 1685 to 1815 in Europe is known as the Enlightenment—an intellectual movement that emphasized reason and skepticism and gave rise to the scientific method. Enlightenment thinkers believed in testing assumptions, subjecting facts to a rigorous process of experimentation, and not believing something just because it seemed reasonable or someone else wanted you to believe it. Enlightenment ideals and the understanding of science in the 1700s certainly contributed to the decline in witchcraft allegations in Europe, but these ideals hadn't yet reached North America in 1692.

What if just one of the judges on the Court of Oyer and Terminer had demanded the type of proof that we'd accept today to show the afflicted girls' fits were caused by witchcraft? Or that the "touch test" worked? Many accusations were made for revenge, but some were based on utter bewilderment about why a cow had died in a weird position or a cider keg had suddenly gone dry.

In 1976 Dr. Linnda Caporael suggested another possible cause for the afflicted girls' fits: *ergotism*. Ergot is a fungus that grows on grain, especially rye, that's gotten wet. If you eat bread made from grain contaminated by ergot, you'll have hallucinations and possibly convulsions. Sounds a lot like Abigail and Betty's symptoms, doesn't it? And the summer of 1691 had been wet, so bread made from grain harvested at that time and eaten in the late winter of 1692 could well have had the fungus.

It's a fascinating theory, but most scholars today don't believe it. For one thing, there were two other children besides Abigail and Betty living in the Parris household; why weren't *they* affected? Ann Putnam had younger siblings; didn't any of them eat bread? Another issue with ergotism as an explanation is that some of the symptoms in Salem were very clearly faked. People didn't shove pins in their knees because of a fungus, and ergotism doesn't cause you to bite your own wrist.

As people began to understand more of the scientific principles that underpin the world, they saw natural laws at work more often and fewer witches flying by night. The transition to an age of science is especially visible in the work of Reverend Cotton Mather long after the witch trials. In 1713 Mather lost his wife and three of his children to measles. Eight years later, Boston had a terrible smallpox epidemic in which many people died. Mather knew the work of an English doctor who'd observed that people who survived smallpox didn't get it again, and from this insight, the idea of inoculating against the disease was born—giving people a very early version of a smallpox vaccine.

Reverend Mather strongly supported the effort to control smallpox and inoculated his own son against the disease, then began a highly public campaign to persuade other people to protect their families, too. Not everyone agreed with his efforts; someone threw a homemade bomb through his window in protest against his push for inoculations! Reverend Mather turned out to be right, though. This man who'd once applauded the execution of witches convicted on spectral evidence became a champion of evidence-based medical advances. The world was slipping forward.

I bet you think it left me behind—that I may talk about "our world today," but I'm not in it. There's no Thomas Putnam now. The world of the witch trials is long gone. If that's what you think, you're wrong. I've been trying to warn you. Even in an age that understands science, hysteria and false allegations can take hold and grow shockingly fast. And the farther they get before someone stands up to demand proof, the harder they are to stop. Is our current age of disinformation and AI and deepfake videos all that different from a Salem in which rumors of the Devil spread from lip to ear? Our age is safer only if we make it that way.

What can we learn from the witch trials? Be aware of danger, but don't be terrified. Fear hung like fog over Salem, and like fog, it made it hard to see clearly. If someone makes an accusation, ask to see the evidence. Just because one thing happens and then another thing happens doesn't mean the first thing *caused* the second thing. You need to be able to show a *connection*. Don't mistake a pimple for a witch's mark; pimples are embarrassing enough as it is. And always, be kind.

Because if we don't believe in evidence and reason and kindness, there's nothing that says neighbors can't turn once more against neighbors. Or that I can't rise again.

I am the Hanging Tree.

And I'm waiting.

ROLL CALL OF THE DEAD

NAME	CAUSE OF DEATH	DATE
SARAH OSBORNE	died in jail	May 10, 1692
BRIDGET BISHOP	hanged	June 10, 1692
ROGER TOOTHAKER	died in jail	June 16, 1692
INFANT OF SARAH GOOD	died in jail	sometime before July 19, 1692
SARAH GOOD	hanged	July 19, 1692
ELIZABETH HOWE	hanged	July 19, 1692
SUSANNAH MARTIN	hanged	July 19, 1692
REBECCA NURSE	hanged	July 19, 1692
SARAH WILDES	hanged	July 19, 1692
GEORGE BURROUGHS	hanged	August 19, 1692
MARTHA CARRIER	hanged	August 19, 1692
GEORGE JACOBS SR.	hanged	August 19, 1692

JOHN PROCTOR	hanged	August 19, 1692
JOHN WILLARD	hanged	August 19, 1692
GILES COREY	pressed to death	September 19, 1692
MARTHA COREY	hanged	September 22, 1692
MARY ESTY	hanged	September 22, 1692
ALICE PARKER	hanged	September 22, 1692
MARY PARKER	hanged	September 22, 1692
ANN PUDEATOR	hanged	September 22, 1692
WILMOTT REDD	hanged	September 22, 1692
MARGARET SCOTT	hanged	September 22, 1692
SAMUEL WARDWELL	hanged	September 22, 1692
DOG #1	shot	October 1692
DOG #2	shot	October 1692
ANN FOSTER	died in jail	December 3, 1692
LYDIA DUSTIN	died in jail	March 10, 1693

AUTHOR'S NOTE

The events in Salem occurred in 1692 and 1693. The Julian calendar was in effect then. It had been devised by Roman emperor Julius Caesar and was off by about eleven minutes a year; after a few centuries of that, it began to add up. The Gregorian calendar is the one we use today. It's more accurate, but it wasn't until 1752 that the British empire—including the colonists in North America—changed to the Gregorian calendar. The discrepancy at that point was eleven days. That's why if you look up John Adams's birth date, for example, you'll see that he was born on October 19, 1735 "Old Style" and October 30, 1735 "New Style." Everyone born before 1752 suddenly had two birthdays. Twice the number of parties? We can only hope.

Of course, this also means that if you look up what day of the week something happened during Salem's witchcraft craze, it won't match what the day of the week actually was for people living through those events. I have boldly called a day "Tuesday" if it was Tuesday for the people living through it. I also modernized spelling and punctuation somewhat for clarity when quoting examination and trial records. You're welcome.

P.S. I'm sorry about the dogs. I always said I'd never kill a dog in a book and here I've killed two. That's the Devil's fault, not mine; please don't hold it against me.

ACKNOWLEDGMENTS

This was a hard book to write. That is partly because the Salem witchcraft records are both sprawling and incomplete, but mostly it's because the events themselves were so horrifying. Some people made it easier, and I'm grateful. My agent, Kate McKean, has the serenity of Rebecca Nurse and the tenacity of Giles Corey. Pam Bobowicz got me started on Salem, Emma D. Dryden did much of the heavy lifting, and Cheryl Klein got us over the finish line. Nick Thornborrow did the illustrations, which I adore. The rest of the team at Workman did their usual stellar job: Lourdes Ubidia, Kim Daly, Jules Kelly, Laura Lutz, Amanda Trautmann, and Alyssa Cuevas.

I'm grateful to historian Geoffrey Parker for the discussions of the Little Ice Age and witchcraft, and for all the laughter. John Robert McFarland and Helen Karr McFarland took us to Salem when I was four and I remember it vividly. Thanks for that. Mary Beth McFarland has always been my biggest supporter, despite the Bunny Slipper Incident. Still sorry! In the evenings my husband, Patrick Kennedy, washed the dishes and listened to my indignant explanations of what happened at Salem, even though he already knew. Thanks, Boogums. To Brigid and Joe, who make the world a better place: I love you.

And to the victims of the Salem witch hunt: Rest in peace.

FURTHER READING

YOUTH

Aronson, Marc, and Stephanie Anderson. *Witch-Hunt: Mysteries of the Salem Witch Trials*. NY: Atheneum Books for Young Readers, 2005.

Gilman, Sarah. *The Salem Witch Trials (Explore Colonial America)*. NY: Enslow Publishing, 2017.

Holub, Joan. *What Were the Salem Witch Trials?* NY: Grosset & Dunlap, 2015.

Schanzer, Rosalyn. *Witches! The Absolutely True Tale of Disaster in Salem*. Washington, D.C.: National Geographic Society, 2011.

Yolen, Jane. *The Salem Witch Trials: An Unsolved Mystery from History*. NY: Simon & Schuster, 2004.

ADULT

Baker, Emerson W. *A Storm of Witchcraft: The Salem Trials and the American Experience*. Oxford: Oxford University Press, 2015.

Daniels, Bruce C. *Puritans at Play: Leisure and Recreation in Colonial New England*. NY: St. Martin's Griffin, 1995.

Demos, John. *The Enemy Within: 2,000 Years of Witch-Hunting in the Western World*. NY: Viking, 2008.

Dow, George Francis. *Every Day Life in the Massachusetts Bay Colony*. NY: Dover Publications, Inc., 1988.